JESUS
INSURGENCY

Rudy Rasmus
Dottie Escobedo-Frank

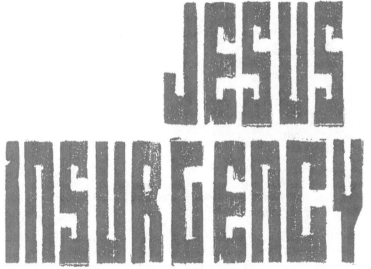

JESUS INSURGENCY

THE CHURCH REVOLUTION FROM THE EDGE

Abingdon Press
Nashville

JESUS INSURGENCY: THE CHURCH REVOLUTION FROM THE EDGE

This book is printed on acid-free paper

Library of Congress Cataloging-in-Publication Data

Escobedo-Frank, Dottie.
 Jesus insurgency : the church revolution from the edge / Dottie Escobedo-Frank and Rudy Rasmus.
  p. cm.
 Includes bibliographical references (p.   ).
 ISBN 978-1-4267-4041-1 (pbk. : alk. paper) 1. Church renewal—United Methodist Church (U.S.) I. Rasmus, Rudy. II. Title.
 BV600.3.E83 2011
 262'.07673—dc23

                    2011035901

Scripture quotations unless otherwise indicated are from the Common English Bible. Copyright © 2011 by the Common English Bible. All rights reserved. Used by permission. (www.CommonEnglishBible.com)

"My City Of Ruins" by Bruce Springsteen. Copyright © 2001 Bruce Springsteen (ASCAP). Reprinted by permission. International copyright secured. All rights reserved.

11 12 13 14 15 16 17 18 19 20—10 9 8 7 6 5 4 3 2 1

MANUFACTURED IN THE UNITED STATES OF AMERICA

Every day, pastors roll out of bed and put their hearts on the line. They love when it is not returned, they give when they feel depleted, they bring hope when it feels hopeless, and they preach the gospel whether or not they see change. Pastors courageously bring God's love to the world and are continuously faithful to their calling. They are the underground swell of the church's revolution.

The pastor's life is the most depressing and the most joyful life. The two exist side by side and in tension with each other.

To us, Rudy and Dottie, pastors are heroes. We honor you, the pastor, for the depth of your love. And we dedicate this book to every moment of your call.

CONTENTS

Chapter 1. At the Crossroads   1

Signposts of Death and Decline   4
One Church at the Crossroads   7
The Greater Church Crossroads   11
The Path of Life and The Path of Death   21
Choosing the Path of Life   28

Chapter 2. The Insurgent   35

The Insurgent   35
A Jesus Insurgency . . .   45
Naming the Insurgents   48
Insurgents Live a New Way . . . the Way of Love   52

Chapter 3. The Church Revolution   59

The View from the Street   60
A Revolution Is Different from an Insurgency   66
Abusive Power   67
Revolutionary Places   74

Chapter 4. From the Edge   89

Change Happens from the Edge   89
The Creative Church   94
The Maverick Future Church   105
Onward Christian Church   106
Postscript   110

Notes   113

CHAPTER 1

AT THE CROSSROADS

Dottie Escobedo-Frank

We stand at a crossroads.

The church is, at this very moment, in the middle of epochal change. We are dying, if not already dead, and our future is no longer in the hands of positional leaders. There is an insurgency rising up. It is a church revolution that you may not have heard of, because it is happening way out on the edge. The church is now in the hands of insurgents and revolutionaries, the young and the outcasts, the sarcastics and the irreverents. It is up to these people—the people on the edge—to lead the church toward hope and life. Perhaps you have sensed it too.

My road is winding. I grew up Lutheran, the daughter of Lutheran pastors and missionaries to Mexico, and I love my Lutheran roots. As an adult, I became a United Methodist because my husband, the son of an Assemblies of God pastor, could not handle the Lutheran liturgy. We found a common bond in The Methodist Church, and love the Methodist way and its Wesleyan theology of grace. Over time I became a

1

mother, then a social worker, then, eventually, a pastor. Each of these roads is a part of my journey.

Currently I serve a church called CrossRoads. The name is fitting. The church sits literally at the crossroads of Central and Northern Avenue in Phoenix, Arizona. Some people come to this church because they see the name as they drive by, and they take it as a sign from God. Knowing they are at their own life crossroads, they stop in to see what God has to say to them. I love that.

Our name fits for a deeper reason too. Our church is living at a crossroads, just like that which is occurring in churches all over America. It is the juncture of life and death. It is the place where one stands and looks around—north, south, east, and west— and makes a life-changing determination on which way to go forward. Many churches come to this intersection point and just inch along in the same direction, oblivious that they just encountered three (or more) alternate routes to being the church in God's world. They ignore the signs and walk toward death simply because that's the only path they have ever considered.

Others arrive at the crossroads and recognize that what they are entering into is the valley of the shadow of death. Yet they stay there, hanging on to a slow death process that is both known and inevitable.

It is understandable, really. As a social worker in hospital settings, I witnessed people's knee-jerk reactions to the imminent death of loved ones, as they chose to slow down the inevitable, prolong life, and avoid death, instead of allowing for its natural march to come. I get it. It hurts to see death up close.

Sometimes we even put on the ultimate set of blinders: we keep a body alive even though it is already dead. At our request, doctors keep a person no longer living connected to machines that breathe and pump the heart for him or her, machines that keep a body looking pink and alive even though it is obvious by brain scans and physical exams that the person is already gone. Doctors do it to help a family get ready to receive the news that their loved one is dead, and they do it to prove they have done everything they can, so they don't get sued. It is called "life support," but the body lying on the bed connected to machines is not alive. This is the ultimate push against death. It is an attempt to make it seem that we have the upper hand over death.

After many years of working in hospitals and encountering death weekly, I can tell you that the greater pain is in watching someone you love die a long, agonizing death. And the greater love is one that allows for a death that is less painful, even when more imminent. It puts love of the person experiencing transformation before your own comfort. When the death process occurs naturally and without intervention, it creates a memory of peace. When we have the courage to stay at the deathbed without prolonging pain, we get to see the experience of the "window of heaven." We see death as a glimpse into the realm of the eternal.

The conventional church has been hanging around the crossroads of Graveyard and Decision Street for a few decades, without acknowledging that the location is death. We have chosen to inch along, ignoring a world that has changed. We have ignored the lack of young people in our midst. We have not acknowledged that we are almost all white. We have ignored the absence of new believers in our midst. We have sent our money "over there" and patted ourselves on the back, ignoring the homeless and hungry next door. We have allowed other agencies to do our charitable, missional work for us. We have continued to live in the Industrial Age, ignoring a culture that is now two ages beyond. We have dug our hole deep, yet pretend that we are alive and well. We can't decide whether to live or die, so we hang out on life support.

There is a traditional United Methodist hymn titled "And Are We Yet Alive." It is normative to sing it as a start for our annual gatherings. The title is the central question of the greater church. It is our custom to consider this question of life (or not) at every annual gathering. By "consider" I mean we sing the song, therefore asking the question, but we don't take time to wrestle with the answer. We just move on to the business of the church. I used to say the answer to that question was a resounding yes. But now, I just don't know. We are perhaps barely alive, but we have *fighting without and fears within*—or maybe today we have *fighting within and fears without.* The dissension is so loud it's becoming difficult to hear the grace. Are we alive, church? Or are we bones pretending to have flesh, blood, and soul?

The problem is that the world around the conventional church has changed. Drastically. While the church has been hiding inside the walls for fear of death and decline, the world around has encountered remarkable growth and change. The church, for lack of understanding, has become a fortress, walled-up and caring for its own, alone. We have done it with our structures, our local congregations, and our intimate friendships. We have forgotten to engage God, and we have encountered only ourselves. And for that, we are at a crossroads. For that, we are facing death.

SIGNPOSTS OF DEATH AND DECLINE

Statistics are signs of what has already happened. They are not signs that point us to a future, but signs of a bygone era. When we read statistics, we are analyzing trends that have already occurred. They are our present-past state of being. While many people get excited about statistics, I tend to understand them as exterior and past, and rarely internal and current. So if you know recent church history, the data that follow should feel familiar to you, and will not come as any surprise. (In fact, many books have been written with similar statistical tales of the state of the church.) It is perhaps what you have been living out in your current church. They are signs we have already seen.

In The United Methodist Church in the United States, between 1998 and 2008:

- the average worship attendance declined by 9 percent;

- the number of churches declined by 6 percent;
- the number of baptisms decreased by 31 percent;
- the number of professions of faith decreased by 25 percent;
- the makeup of clergy is 88 percent white and 76 percent male (2008);
- the makeup of church membership is 90 percent white (2008);
- the average age of clergy rose from forty-nine to fifty-four;
- the financial expenditures per member rose 61%; and
- average church costs in 2008 include the following: 36 percent building and debt; 34 percent clergy and lay staffing costs; 20 percent apportionments, benevolence, and programs.[1]

Weekly, forty-three thousand American churchgoers are leaving church, seeking other ways to attend to their spiritual connection. (In The United Methodist Church two thousand leave per week.)[2]

There is more. Pastors, once seen as valued and cherished persons in society, are now experiencing burnout as they lose their place of prominence and encounter the inability to perform the multitude of roles that come with dying and declining congregations. One study by *The Barna Group* looked at the role expectations of pastors and found:

> *fifteen major, diverse responsibilities ranging from management to relationship building to teaching and scholarship. Companion studies indicated that there was no other person in a leadership position—in business, government, education, or non-profit work—expected to master so many and such diverse obligations.*[3]

Too many expectations and roles bring failure and burnout. A study of 963 pastors from The United Methodist Church, the Presbyterian Church (U.S.A.), Evangelical Lutheran Church in America, the Lutheran Church–Missouri Synod, and the Assemblies of God (USA) showed that one-third of pastors left the church.[4] Pastors and lay leaders are experiencing the signs of strain.

A recent *Huffington Post* report had this title: "The World Is Their Parish: Can The United Methodist Church Survive?" It states that newly touted forms of documentation within The UMC structure, called "dashboards," are merely new forms of documenting "maintenance discipleship." Kelly Figueroa-Ray, the author of the article, states:

> *John Wesley, founder of the Methodist movement, was quoted as saying: "The world is my parish." He did not say "the people that show up to this particular building on a Sunday are my parish." The United Methodist Church has become a cushy institution, banking on performance measures kept by fancy gadget dials to help save it from the fate towards which all mainline denominations seem to be heading—slow death.[5]*

The signs are everywhere. And they are not boding well for the church of Jesus Christ. A powerful video called "United Methodist Realities," presented by The UMC's General Council on Finance and Administration at a joint finance meeting for church leaders on pensions and health benefits, drove home the point clearly.[6] It outlines the radical declines in a broad swath of statistical categories since the denominational merger that created The United Methodist Church in 1968.

If you are able, watch the video. I can imagine Jesus in our day, coming to The United Methodist Church and flipping over some tables in righteous anger. I can see his fiery eyes dividing right and wrong inside the church. I can see him turning over the tables of the ways we have sold our souls for a bill of goods that really weren't that "good." I can hear the tremor in his emotion-laden voice as he reminds us, "My Father's house is a house of prayer." I can see a tear fall from his eyes for the state we have gotten into. I don't sense Jesus is pleased right now. And these signposts are shouting, "There's trouble in the garden of God!"

ONE CHURCH AT THE CROSSROADS

The church I serve, CrossRoads United Methodist, is a case in point. Six years ago, it was an aging Anglo congregation of about sixty to one hundred worshipers. Worship attendance mostly hovered in the sixties, but seasonally spiked near one hundred. The pastor before me had worked hard to bring healing to a group of people who experienced pain from the ongoing grief of decades of losing friends who had left the church. The church had been hemorrhaging members for most of their historical memory, and these people grieved the "glory days."

CrossRoads started out as a church in the suburbs, way up north in the grapefruit orchards. With a dynamic young pastor and his wife, it quickly grew to be the magnet for the community, with about one thousand worshipers on a Sunday. When the founding pastor was asked by his bishop to move to another church at the height of CrossRoads's growth, he struggled with the decision, and finally started a new church in another denomination. Most of the one thousand left with him, because he was their pastor. A few hundred remained.

CrossRoads spiraled downward. In the 1980s the church briefly rose when the lay leaders and pastor found a way to engage the neighborhood. Attendance returned to around six hundred. But at the pastor's transfer to another church, which is the United Methodist way, the church's attendance plummeted.

When introduced to the church, the elderly population I first met were those who had seen these two great periods surrounded by decades of decline. At my arrival, the church had experienced more than thirty years of decline. They were still grieving what they perceived as the mass exodus of people they had loved. So to say that CrossRoads was at a crossroads was just stating the reality. It wasn't prophetic. It was apparent.

In the first order of business, we took a step forward and started a new service in a new style of worship. It grew slowly. Five years later, it is larger than the original service, more reflective of the diverse neighborhood around the church, and vibrant in its missional stance. There is still much more room to grow until we are a full house. And when I say "full house," I mean that in more ways than one.

But there has been a battle. We began feeding the homeless population nearby, hosting a ministry called Prodigal's Home, led by Mike and Kim Ricker. The homeless arrived on our campus on Saturday mornings. They were fed a hearty breakfast and given a lively worship service. CrossRoads eventually joined in ministry with Community of Grace Lutheran Church and took on Prodigal's Home as our own ministry. We served together well.

One day, all hell broke loose. The city of Phoenix presented us a cease and desist order, called us a "charity dining hall," and said we were not allowed to feed the homeless hungry on our church property. The news media caught wind of it and told the story of some neighbors fighting against us. Apparently, some vocal neighbors didn't want the homeless from "over there" to come into our neighborhood. (CrossRoads sits on the border of extreme wealth and extreme poverty, and they wanted the line of social demarcation to be maintained.)[7]

But that wasn't half of what was going on. What the press didn't hear was the rest of the story, or maybe I could say, the *real* story: the turmoil and dissension this cease and desist order caused within our own congregation. It was embarrassing enough to have media coverage of dissension between Christian and religious neighbors; what was even more disheartening was the struggle within our church. It almost did us in.

In retrospect, I can see that feeding the homeless was the vehicle that brought the internal problems of our congregation out of hiding and into the light. The essential problem was simply this: some people were fearful of the changes that were happening (and didn't want to do anything that might make the neighbors mad), and others were trying to live out their lives as followers of Jesus Christ in the best way they could, including feeding the hungry of our neighborhood. This event exposed a deep division in the church. It was a clash of cultural time zones: the culture of the past and the culture of the present-future.

There was more. The greater institutional structure of The United Methodist Church assisted as we fought the city of Phoenix. They gave some funds and offered support. But at some point, as the real costs increased, support waned. The cost was literally too much to pursue supporting a prolonged and highly visible legal battle, and the denominational structure could not financially support one church at the expense of many others. This was an understandably difficult decision for any church structure to make, and yet one that let this local church know that the reality of priorities is for the local church to support the structure and not the other way around. It was the first time I saw the limitations of our "connectionalism." The view saddened me and depleted the reserve of spiritual and emotional energy out of which we were operating.

Ultimately, CrossRoads settled with the city of Phoenix. The Rickers made the decision to take Prodigal's Home back to the neighborhood of poverty, 1.5 miles north of the church. The neighbors who had complained were happy. Our settlement agreement was finalized with an agreement that CrossRoads United Methodist Church could feed the hungry in the future (just not this particular group of homeless hungry), and that we would not be cited, or fined, or disallowed to have food at any gatherings. The issue was swept under the rug. Many say it was a defeat for the church. Others called it a win. I say it was both. But not in the way you'd expect.

The defeat was that one group of homeless people did not have the backing of the church to remain free to be fed on church property. They were symbolically rejected. It told them they were not that valuable in the church's eyes. They learned that wealthy people were acceptable on church grounds, and that they were not acceptable. They learned that our "love" was limited by funding, by city codes, and by fear. That is a mighty defeat. It must've made Jesus cry.

The win was that the church, and the church structure, were fully exposed for who we are. No more hiding. No more pretending. The ugliness reared its big head, and we all saw it in our very own midst. The offender was looking at us in the mirror. And that's the win. Because, if you can't see your own problem, there is no way you are going to have the courage to deal with it. Without seeing and acknowledging our failings, there's no way we are going to be able to find a new way. There's no way we are going to be able to fight the good fight of being the love of Jesus in our world. We did many things right as we stood with those who were in great need, but the truth is, we saw the depth of division and the boundaries in our love.

There was one more incidental but significant win. Our whole neighborhood and city (and in fact, other parts of the world) began to talk about who we can feed, and where people can eat. We had major discussions around the questions "Who is my neighbor?" and "Where are homeless allowed to be? Is this a free country for them too?" We forthrightly debated our understanding of the story of the good Samaritan. It was told over and over again and interpreted a thousand ways. During this time, I was often "found" by a reporter wherever I went, which was a disconcerting experience for an introvert like myself. They wanted my (and in essence, the church's) take on neighborliness versus danger. I gave them what information I could, in small sound bites that sometimes made it on the news.

And if you think about it, this is good news! When we are talking about "Who is my neighbor?" this is good news—even when we are disagreeing. At least we are engaging in worthy conversation. (I can remember various heated discussions in the church over things like what color to paint the walls or the placement of the communion cups. This was definitely a better conversation to have.)

One day I was at a restaurant with a friend having lunch. I overheard the table next to me mention "Pastor Dottie." Now, not many people have the name Dottie anymore, and even fewer have "Pastor" attached to it. And so my ears perked up and I listened in. They were having a lively conversation about whether or not our church should feed the homeless on our property. Were we acting like a charity dining hall or like a church when we fed the hungry? They debated back and forth, and really, I enjoyed hearing their discussion from both sides. After we finished our meal and began to leave, I walked over to the table and introduced myself as Pastor Dottie. There was nervous laughter, and a few of them turned pale. I told them they were having a great discussion and to keep it up.

The buzz that we generated for caring for the "least of these" in our own backyards versus "over there" was a definite win.

But as I sit on the resolution side of a crazy, painful, difficult situation within my particular local church, I see the great loss we all face. CrossRoads is not unique to church fights. We had Sundays when the police showed up to ask neighbors to leave us alone while we worshiped, with one officer telling me all the while, "This is why I don't go to church. Don't get me wrong, Pastor, I believe in Jesus. But I want nothing to do with church for this very reason." All I could do was apologize for the church, and tell the police officer it is not supposed to be like this. We are not unique to internal dissension. It began in the days of the New Testament, and it continues to the present. But what is alarming is that we have focused on the wrong thing. We are focused on getting our way. We are self-centered congregations. We are a nation of self-absorbed "Christians" both at the local church level and in the wider structural arena.

This is the same division that the conventional church faces today. Will we stand at the crossroads of decision and put the brakes on, remaining in the place of sure but slow death? Or will we opt for the harder choice of transformation, facing the uncertainties of the future with courage, hope, and faith?

This has been the story of my particular church, but let's look also at the greater church.

THE GREATER CHURCH CROSSROADS

Consider the following blog entry, titled "Ten Reasons Why Your Church Sucks."

1. It does not understand the community at large.
2. It has poor leadership.

3. It has no solid vision.
4. It is graying, quickly.
5. It's inbred.
6. It's concerned with look and not action.
7. It's comfortable in its misery, and is looking for company.
8. It's out of touch with the 21st century.
9. It's all about money.
10. It's all politics.[8]

The church is in trouble, a heap of trouble. We are at the bottom of the bell curve, in danger of death, and at a place where we need to reconsider what we are about. If we take some wisdom from the business world, we could look at ourselves from the perspective of reality. Marc Andreessen, the founder and former CEO of Netscape, wrote "Ten Reasons We're Going to Go Out of Business."[9] He encourages businesses to take the time to script out their own ten reasons why you're going to go out of business. The exercise sheds light into the dark corners of companies. Inspired by that, I painfully imagined the following:

TEN REASONS WHY THE UMC IS DYING

1. A focus on top-heavy structure instead of making disciples of Jesus Christ.
2. A preference for traditionalism and a negative attitude toward innovation.
3. A welfare mentality within the professional clergy and bishops, fostered by the itinerant system, pension fund, and continual moves.
4. Funds spent on the institutional structure instead of on fresh moves of the Holy Spirit.
5. A punitive system of leadership based on control and authoritative permission-giving.
6. A hierarchical, closed system of outdated communication tools in an open-source communication world.

7. Worship wars and worship that does not connect with culture.
8. Mission to the wealthy and not to the disenfranchised.
9. A loss of focus on grace and compassion and a split between extreme conservative and liberal views.
10. We forgot Jesus.

These issues are at the crossroads of death. They are also the place where God's resurrection possibilities exist.

THE DIVIDED CHURCH

We are so divided that our very reputation propels people away from the way of Christ. People wonder why we have to have so many denominations. (According to David Barrett, George T. Kurian, and Todd M. Johnson, there are 33,830 Christian denominations.[10]) They can't explain the differences, but they feel the divide. People today hear Christians fighting over all kinds of social wars (abortion, conservative and liberal politics, homosexuality, and immigration), and they think that we are merely a fighting club. They see us as narrow-minded and phobic (homophobe, femmephobe, ethniphobe, povertyphobe, and so on). People today think Christians talk what they are afraid to walk, while most people would rather do the walk even if they can't explain the talk. The world around the church is not impressed by the state of the church.

The divisions among Christians today are more about ways of being Christian than they are about polity or theology. Luke Timothy Johnson says, "The challenge to Christians today is to embrace a catholicity of religious sensibility and expression rather than to divide on the basis of mutual suspicion of ways of being Christian that seem strange."[11]

So if we have moved away from disagreeing about our polity and our theology, then what is it that the world sees?

They see that we have not embraced a catholicity of religious sensibility and expression.[12] To put it simply, people looking at Christianity from the outside in do not see the core of the church getting along as a general principle of acceptance, and they watch us fight over the expression of our faith. And so, unimpressed, they pass on Christianity after seeing this kind of living. They take note that we don't even seem to like one another. We call ourselves "Christians," but there is confusion about what that means. Surely it is enough to be "spiritual but not religious." Outsiders think, "Surely our way is the better way." This is the state the church, the bride of Christ, finds itself in.

The original dream of the Methodists was simple: create a free-flowing structure that allowed for movement, innovation, and growth. But the current state of The United Methodist Church is a complex, stifling structure that prevents change by hierarchical strangulation of innovation, movement, and growth. The original dream was lead by lay pastors, pastors, and lay leaders; the current structure is led by professional clergy, bishops, and structural bureaucrats. The original hope for evangelism followed the movement of the Holy Spirit to frontiers, fields, and places where the populace naturally gathered; the current state of outreach involves performing cultural tricks to attract people into strongholds of claimed but deserted territory. The original dream for growing faithful followers of Jesus Christ in discipleship connected individuals into small accountability groups where people were invited to deepen their faith in, and love for, God and God's people; the current state of discipleship is haphazard and even nonexistent in many churches. The original dream of the connectional structure in the Methodist movement was to provide support and a greater mission field; the current state of the connection includes obtaining resources from the local churches to hold up and support the top-heavy structure of the institution. The original dream of the Methodist movement included the poor and outcasts in the life and leadership of the church; the current state mainly gathers Anglo, wealthy, aging, and highly educated uniform groups of people who see the poor as "the other" or "those needing help." And finally, the original Methodist movement grew like wildfire across England and the new frontier lands of America. The current state is a burning ember—some say a bed of ashes—hoping to be enflamed and reborn with the love of our Lord Jesus.

The United Methodist Church and the mainline churches as a whole have traveled a long way from their original fires of genius. The original dream for the Presbyterians was a dream free from church hierarchy and squarely centered in the Scriptures. The original dream for Lutherans was to bring the word of God and the location of the gospel into the hands of the people and away from the control of the priests. The original dream for the Episcopalians came from a revolution in a new land, and a choice to give allegiance to the future. The original dream for the United Church of Christ was to be a place where all could worship and gather freely and without condemnation, where true love would rule the day.

The original dream for the disciples was to take the good news of the resurrection of Jesus Christ to the whole world.

It is time to remember our origins and fan into flames the love of Jesus Christ. It is time for a new rise of Jesus-followers to form an insurgent, insistent movement of grace.

THE UNITED METHODIST CALL TO ACTION

The United Methodist Church is recognizing its need for change and has formed a Call to Action Steering Team, led by Bishop Gregory Palmer and the Council of Bishops. The team was courageous in their willingness to look at the church transparently, and to advocate the needed change, knowing that this change will affect the lives and jobs of many people they know and love, including, of course, themselves. I commend them for their courage. This committee gathered information from across the country, and stated their hope for the future and present as "dreams of a church with more grace and freedom and fewer rules—more accountability to the gospel and less conformity to an outdated, bureaucratic system; more ministry with the poor and less reticence to link arms with the desperate, the sick and the hungry; more dreaming about what will be and less struggling to preserve what was; and more trust and less cynicism."[13]

What the world sees currently as "church" is not what the disciples of Jesus Christ hoped for. The original Methodist Church was formed in a short, ten-day gathering called *The Christmas Conference.* The *Discipline* and doctrine were formed as guidelines for itinerant preachers who had little time to check out the rules as they traveled by horseback between church locations. The structure was simple, practical, and supportive.

A new call to focus The United Methodist Church was written by various bishops and addressed in Scott Jones and Bruce Ough's *The Future of the United Methodist Church: Seven Vision Pathways.* The seven pathways of focus include:

1. Planting New Congregations
2. Transforming Existing Congregations
3. Teaching the United Methodist Way
4. Strengthening Clergy and Lay Leadership
5. Children and Poverty
6. Expanding Racial/Ethnic Ministries
7. Eliminating Poverty by Stamping out Disease[14]

These pathways are a step in the right direction, as one hopes to transform church in the local context. What the pathways do not address is how to deconstruct (and therefore reform) a costly and often ineffective administration of the greater church. While the pathways directives can be addressed mostly locally, Methodist churches are spending an inordinate amount of resources to hold together an obese structure. What the local churches need is structural weight loss.

While the stated mission of The United Methodist Church is "to make disciples of Jesus Christ for the transformation of the world,"[15] the problem is that our current structure prevents our mission from becoming reality. It is weighty, heavy, and a burden to bear for local churches, local pastors, and leaders. Now is the time to focus on making disciples and turn to look toward the possibility of a simple, streamlined, supportive structure that makes way for creativity to flourish and provides an imaginative solution out of the current crisis.

The Call to Action of The United Methodist Church calls for a new definition of life. "Vital Churches," it says, are those that will, in the near and well-documented future, score on these indicators:

1. Churches will have both traditional and contemporary worship gatherings.
2. Churches will have many small groups.
3. Churches will have many programs for youth and children.
4. Churches will be led by pastors who are great at preaching and at planning.
5. Churches will be diligent to place more laypeople in leadership roles.[16]

While these factors are all well and good, it seems we have not learned from our very recent past mistakes. A recent, well-publicized study by Willow Creek Church called *REVEAL* looked at the question of whether church activities helped to make for spiritual growth. Their answer? A resounding no![17]

So while this study is still fresh on our minds, we choose to repeat the same mistake by calling for more programs, more activities, and more worshiping formats. Since when did God bless our programs and speak to us in our whirlwind? God spoke most often in the whisper, the quiet, the center of the storm (1 Kings 19:11-13). We humans forget that when things are not working, it is time to stop and rest and listen. We tend to do more of the same, and faster, hoping our frantic activities will somehow bring different results.

The Call to Action is an attempt to save the dying institution we know as The United Methodist Church. It attempts to do so by scoring our losses (general agencies and the Council of Bishops scored "below average") and changing our focus to the local church (which scored "average"). And then it attempts to define "vital congregations" with markers that can be counted and reported. This new accounting system will somehow save the church?

The two independent studies were completed. One study came up with the Five Vital Church Indicators listed above; the other graded our current operation and structures. The studies concluded that we are failing ("below average") on structural abilities to make disciples of Jesus Christ, and are only average in doing this at the local church level. Our structures are costly and do not produce desired results. We are spending too much on episcopal salaries, clergy salaries, and building maintenance (per member). And we are failing (below average) on resolving conflicts across the church. The report had a foundational conclusion: "The support structure of the U.S. Church has been precipitously turned on its head; we have fewer failing to support more. The Church simply cannot afford to support itself for much longer without drastic change."[18]

While the church structure is failing to be a supportive fortress, the local church is also doing poorly. The study shows that we are spending too much money on too many clergy for too few churches.[19]

One other problem related to clergy and churches is the fact that we are, as of 2008,

- predominantly "white" (88 percent) and male (76 percent) clergy;
- predominantly "white" (90 percent) membership; and
- the average clergy age was fifty-four, up from forty-nine in 1998.[20]

It is a long, prohibitive, and extremely expensive process to become a pastor, and young people are choosing other denominations to follow their call. Once you become a clergy member, the expectations and load on the clergy are so outrageous that "clergy cannot please anyone—clergy are trapped between 'system' and 'congregation.'"[21]

The report states that the clergy are the "front line" for making disciples of Jesus Christ, yet they are not supported by structure, by role, or by process.[22] Further, they are not supported by local church leadership, but rather are expected to perform all tasks related to the church from typing up bulletins and cleaning toilets to setting vision and making disciples. The load on the clergy is soul breaking. And the support for the clergy is minuscule. Meanwhile, we spend dollars, time, and effort on the boards and agencies that are failing to support the local church where the most (but not many) disciples of Jesus Christ are being made.[23]

The church is at a major crossroads, and if more of the same is the clarion call for transformation, then we are in a very deep mess. And really, folks, it doesn't smell pretty.

PRIESTHOOD OF ALL BELIEVERS?

Kenneth Carder reminds us that much of the greatness of Wesley was his involvement of the laity in the leadership of the church. He states,

> This began with his realization that he could not rely upon ordained clergy in achieving his goal of "spreading scriptural holiness across the land." . . . Wesley sought out the least noticeable, including the poor, and helped to form them into influential leaders of classes and societies.[24]

In the original Methodist movement, lay leadership was central. People in the congregation would gather weekly to discuss their spiritual lives and love for Jesus Christ. These class meetings held people accountable, provided support, and gave leadership of the church into the hands of the laity. The clergy visited a circuit of churches, but the weekly moments of a community were lay led. The ownership of the church, clearly in the hands of the people, was not about numbers or statistics, but about growing souls in love with God. Today The UMC and the "Call to Action" are calling for accountability to rise again—only now this accountability is in the hands of the bishops. Bishops and the institutional structure have become the central forces, while the church has forgotten the necessary role of the local church, the pastors, and the laity. These decisions, I fear, are once again more of the same.

Rev. Steve Manskar, director of Wesleyan leadership for the United Methodist Board of Discipleship, believes that putting the church in the hands of the laity is of utmost importance. He states, "That's where the revival is going to come from. We need to have laity taking the lead in the visiting, the caring and the mission of the church."[25]

The church today has lost its focus on laity leading the way. And so, instead, the laity lead in the only way they are allowed—by *dissension*. Maybe you have heard this: "It's time for this pastor to leave" or "I won't support this particular church council if they don't go in the direction we've always gone" or "I'll withhold my check until things go my way." Perhaps this type of leadership occurs out of the memory of times past when lay leadership was a vital, central, and necessary part of the church. Instead, today churches often experience frequent pastoral moves and the correlated congregational patterns of switching churches, with accompanying dissatisfaction and distrust in the pastor or the institution: "Why should we pay toward the structure? What has the system ever done for us?" The laity fights and squabbles, looking for a place to lead. A negative response is better than no response at all.

The truth is, the laity has been held back by the professionalism of the clergy and the hierarchical process of the institution. If the laity took hold of real leadership by leading the classes, by visiting the sick, by becoming involved in relationship with the poor and outcasts of their town, then the church could become what it was meant to be: a place where every believer is a priest. Then we would not be defined as "clergy" and "laity," but as *claity*, a melding of leadership to provide the new clay pot for this day.

THE PATH OF LIFE AND THE PATH OF DEATH

The church is at a crossroads. She has a choice to walk down the path of life or the path of death. The church has to choose. You have to choose. While you may be thinking that you don't have to make a choice, we all know that "no choice" is a choice. It is the choice of stagnation and eventual death. Eugene Peterson, in *A Long Obedience in the Same Direction*, states, "There is always a way that leads out of distress—a way that begins in repentance, or turning to God."[26]

When we choose the way of Christ, we choose to lose ourselves at the foot of the cross. We choose to repent and change our ways; to be willing to die to self so that the world can live a new life of grace, mercy, and hope. This is our individual choice, but the church must do the same. But in our effort to choose the path of least resistance, we have forgotten to choose the hard way. Our comfort seems to be what we have inherited, without contemplation or reflection. Our way seems right because it is what we know. It is only when our comfortable way becomes obviously problematic that we question its correctness. People are only willing to change when the perceived pain of the current crisis exceeds the perceived pain of adaptation to change.[27]

So we must be willing to die. And we must acknowledge our own death. Our structures, our traditions, our preferences, our way of being, and our control must be set free to die. Andrew Root, in *The Promise of Despair*, says that while our world is intent on avoiding death, there is a secret that the church must acknowledge. This secret says that

> *if we will despair, if we will be willing to face death, if we will bear reality, we will discover an amazing paradox, an amazing reality: that the God of life through the Incarnation, Crucifixion, and Resurrection has made death and despair the very location of God's being. . . . God is found in the despair of the cross. God is found in our many deaths, bringing possibility out of nothingness.*[28]

Is the church willing to go to the cross and to face death in order to watch God bring us life? Death is a brutal reality, and not one to be romanticized. When someone I love dies, my grief is strong, life changing, and hard to bear. I know death. I watched my infant daughter die, and I have stood at the bedside of many people who died simply and courageously. Truly, as a pastor and social worker, I know that when a mother goes to the graveside and kneels down on the earth to peer into the hole that will be her child's physical home, she is in deep despair. When I have watched a mom attempt to crawl down into the hole with her dead child, I understand the desire to cross over to the other side to avoid the coming pain and grief. So I don't say this lightly, but with the full understanding of the deepest pain that death can bring. It is real, and it is a wound that takes a long time to heal.

Yet this is our central story: the story of death and resurrection. Is the church ready to be so much like Christ that we allow for death? Again, Root says, "The reformation of the church, then, does not start with ideas and actions alone. . . . Rather, it starts with the bravery to enter into the despair of death, with the audacity to seek the God of life in the deaths in our world and in ourselves."[29]

Root says it is there, at death and at the cross, that we encounter God. God meets us at the place of our greatest need, at the place of our deepest hopelessness, and at our graveyards. And God meets us there to bring us to life. The path of life and death are closely related. Life comes through death. It cannot happen without it.

Romans speaks to this death as well:

> Or don't you know that all who were baptized into Christ Jesus were baptized into his death? Therefore we were buried together with him through baptism into his death, so that just as Christ was raised from the dead through the glory of the Father, we too can walk in newness of life. (Romans 6:3-4)

The Scriptures remind us that parts of our lives, and by extension, parts of the church, will die. It is not for nothing. It is for life, and it is for the future, and it is for those who have not yet heard the good news of the love of Jesus.

There are two kinds of death: death that ends life, and death that births life. We have to make the choice between *death and death* and *death and life*. Death *and* life are what we are striving for. But we are often held back.

DEATH AND DEATH: THE GUARDS

The church has fought death since the disciples argued with Jesus when he was trying to prepare them for his. The Guards hope to delay death.

The business world has written much about the need for, and path toward, change. Robert Quinn, in his book *Deep Change*, discusses the difference between "deep change" and "slow death." "Slow death" is what occurs when we choose the status quo over the option of "deep change."[30] Quinn describes how we often choose to hide behind the facts, pretend that our situation is not that bad, and generally allow the slow death to occur, by our acts of omission and lack of engagement in solutions. This withdrawal, burnout, and avoidance behavior is choosing slow death. Quinn states that we generally choose slow death over the alternative of growth, and we choose it because it is what we know.[31] He also reminds us that death and resurrection are parts of life, but that "only when our pain gets excruciating are we willing to humble ourselves and consider new actions that might allow us to successfully progress in our new situation."[32]

Churches, like businesses, often choose "slow death" as a default. Because change is so difficult, and because it takes more than surface change to make a difference when death is near, churches often opt to live in decline. It takes heroic effort to face the price of pain, and even more so when congregations are elderly and facing their own physical pain of letting go of life itself.

The truth of the matter is that we are a church that is born to live out our central story: the story of the death and resurrection of Jesus Christ. We love to incorporate resurrection stories into our narrative, but we hesitate, and downright avoid the stories of *death* that brings life. But the Scripture says:

> *Look, fool! When you put a seed into the ground, it doesn't come back to life unless it dies. What you put in the ground doesn't have the shape that it will have, but it's a bare grain of wheat or some other seed. God gives it the sort of shape that he chooses, and he gives each of the seeds its own shape. (1 Corinthians 15:36-38)*

The church has repeatedly found ways to go around what it sees as death and create ways to be the living dead. The church still has the mind-set to argue with Jesus, the Christ, about this need to die. It is understandable in an intellectual way, but it is not Christian. Christian churches embrace death-and-life understandings and yield to what God is up to, even when it means the loss of what we know and love.

In our current day, the Guards are protecting the value of slow, painful, rotting, stinking death. They are clinging to crumbling structures, hoping the ultimate crumble doesn't happen in their lifetime. They are leading the church down paths of secular "success," forgetting that the Christlike definition of success is failure. The Guards exist at all levels of the church, from occasional visitor, to lay member, to pastor, to bishop, to agency staff. We all claim to want renewal, and yet we continue to play the role of Guard over What Once Was and Is Now Familiar. The Call to Action started as a courageous act, but if we make the changes merely about what to count, if we become the Guardians of what we know, then we are only delaying the church's inevitable end.

DEATH AND LIFE: THE HOPEFULS

But we have examples of Christ-followers who courageously broke out of the mold and pushed past slow death.

Martin Luther

The story of Martin Luther, a rebel who could no longer tolerate the status quo of the church of his day, is one of death and resurrection. He was willing to lose all—his priesthood, his congregation, his voice, his calling—in order to find the life that welled up within him for bringing the word of God to the common people. So he spoke against the abuses of the church by writing out his *95 Theses*, and he made them public for all to see by nailing them to the church doors. If he had lived in this era, he would have posted them on Facebook or Twitter or his own blog. He did this act of defiance because he was more afraid of losing his soul than he was of losing his place in society. He did this act of defiance because he had a love that went deep and wide, one that spread out into the multitudes of people who needed to know the One he loved, Jesus the Christ. He did this because his understanding of Jesus was broader than the understanding his church promoted.

The first post of the *95 Theses* speaks to our need to turn around in the whole life of the church. It states, "Our Lord and Master Jesus Christ, when He said *Poenitentiam agite*, willed that the whole life of believers should be repentance."[33] And the ninety-fourth and ninety-fifth theses are as follows:

> *94. Christians are to be exhorted that they be diligent in following Christ, their Head, through penalties, deaths, and hell;*
>
> *95. And thus be confident of entering into heaven rather through many tribulations, than through the assurance of peace.*[34]

Luther's passionate call is for the church to repent, reform around Jesus Christ, and not to expect the way of ease.

Luther's *95 Theses* posted on the door of the church in an age where the newfangled printing press spread his word throughout the world with the seed of what Clay Shirky calls "mass amateurization." Luther wanted the Scriptures to be available to the folks on the street, and the mass to be available to all. Shirky states that mass amateurization takes what once belonged to the professionals and makes it available to everyone.[35] Because he spoke his truth and utilized the new communication systems of his day, Luther spread his message and created a mass protest, now called the Protestant Reformation.

Something died for Martin Luther that day. And something was born as well.

John Wesley

John Wesley took cues from what wasn't working in his life to find a new way to live out his understanding of church. He wasn't the most popular preacher in his day. In fact, for a period of time, every time he preached in a church, he was asked to never come back. One day, he accepted an invitation from George Whitefield, with much hesitancy, to preach in the field as miners came off their shift. He had never preached outdoors before. He had never been to the field. But when he spoke, the Spirit filled the hills and the people were moved, and he saw a new way to be church. Wesley fought taking church to the streets much of his life. But one day, seeing the move of the Holy Spirit, he changed his mind. He spent his remaining days caring for the poor and widows and organizing the method of making disciples. He formed groups and clusters and annual gatherings. He used his skills of organization to bring life into the church through small groups of people seeking after God. He never meant for this to be the church, only for it to go alongside the church.

But something happened that Wesley didn't plan. The people's lives were changed. They sought after God and they experienced new life. They attended to their rituals because they were so in love with their Lord. They spread the word across England and then to America. Bit by bit, things changed as the core value of sharing life together in small settings changed the larger church.[36]

At the end of his life, Wesley finally had a church building, artifacts of which are now found in the Foundry Chapel in London, where he was pastor in a local setting. Since he was also an inventor, he helped to design and fashion the pews for this church building. And, believing in the value of people talking to one another, he set the backs of the pews on hinges. The pew backs could be moved from the back of the seat to the front of the seat. On a visit to the Foundry Chapel site in 2005, the guide explained that after Wesley's sermons, the people would reset the backs of the pews so that they could sit in two rows facing each other, and they would discuss the sermon and apply it to their lives. This setup was also used for the class meetings. In the Church of England, this was a radical departure from the staid and set way of being church.

Across the street from the Wesley chapel is Bunhill Fields Cemetery, also called "Dissenter's Cemetery." It became the burial place for the dissenters—those who were seen as non-conformists or who had died outside of the life of the Church of England. It is fascinating to see who is buried there:

> William Blake (1757–1827), poet, and his wife, Catherine (1762–1831)
>
> John Owen (1616–83), Congregational minister
>
> Susanna Wesley (1669–1742), mother of John and Charles Wesley
>
> Daniel Defoe (1661–1731), author of Robinson Crusoe
>
> John Bunyan (1628–88), author of The Pilgrim's Progress—his elaborate tomb includes an effigy of Bunyan and bas-reliefs of scenes from his great allegory
>
> Isaac Watts (1674–1748), hymnwriter
>
> George Fox (1624–91), founder of the Society of Friends (Quakers)—in the Quaker Gardens, next to the Bunhill Fields Meeting House[37]

George Fox, the founder of the Quakers, was known to have written this poem:

> The Papists they cry, Conform.
>
> And the Turk, he cries, Conform.
>
> And did not the heathen Emperors cry, Conform?
>
> And the Presbyterian, he cried, Conform.

And the Independents . . .

So everyone that gets the uppermost, and gets the staff of authority, commands . . .

But no law of Jesus requires it, who said, "Freely you have received, freely give."[38]

For Wesley, and for many other religious visionary leaders, the sacrifice of change was greater than they ever imagined: it had to come with a price. What died was traditionalism. What rose was a fresh move of the Spirit.

What is apparent is that in order for change to happen we must accept and even "lean into" the chaos that brings new life. As Dwight Friesen states, "Embracing life as the dance of chaos with order is an invitation to look for relational patterns in creation and community."[39]

Death is the ultimate chaos, and yet it is part of the order of the universe. Organizations die. People die. Churches die. And yet we live on. The church lives on because it knows the ultimate plan of resurrection and life. And it wills itself to live and die in chaos so that it can live.

CHOOSING THE PATH OF LIFE

The Hopefuls are seeking for the path of life now.

Leonard Sweet reminds the church that the original sign-readers for the birth of Christ were not people within the local religious structure, but that "pagan semioticians were the first to worship the newborn king. Pagans got to Jesus before the holy and righteous."[40]

If we take a lesson from the story of the birth of Jesus, then we can open our eyes to those who live outside the walls of the church and find out what messages God is sending their way. The church can remove hands from her eyes, ears, and mouths, risking exposure to see, hear, or speak something evil, and associate with the rest of God's creation, looking for the places where God might also reside and hearing the words that God continues to make plain. It is arrogant to believe that the only ones God speaks to are people like "us." God speaks to whomever God chooses. And if the church is not seeking, God will make the rocks, and other people groups, to shout out God's praise. Sweet calls the church to move from what we knew in the past to be right and good to what is new and good for the present and future. He says, "Nudgers make the familiar strange. Nudgers overcome the deadening effects of the overfamiliar by reframing familiar things in unfamiliar ways."[41]

Sweet explains this concept further:

> As a literary device, defamiliarization was formulated by the Russians years ago in the concept of ostranenie, which translates literally as "denumbing" and was designed as a distancing device to help the reader see something deadeningly familiar in a totally new light.[42]

The church needs some time to become less familiar with God. We have put God in a box that is "doable" and "knowable." And as such, the church expresses confidence that the God they know is the God that is. In truth, the God that has been allowed into our communities is just a toenail sketch of the vastness of the universe of God. If we learn to let go of the familiar and stop the numbing effect of our routines and rituals, then we might begin to see, hear, and follow God into the world.

We need a time for believing in miracles again, even the miracles of birth. When a baby is born, the whole room is filled with tears and awe and speechlessness at the beauty of a new creation. The church needs some new birth experiences. It would be silenced, and the tears would flow, and the wonder of God would once again be present in our communities. It is time for new birth.

It is essential to remember that "the Gospel—the dunamis of God—is dynamic and not static. It evolves into newer and newer forms in keeping with each local situation and according to the need of the hour."[43]

Our true gospel tradition is the tradition of movement. The early church was as explosive as dynamite. Think about it. The disciples, women and men who spent three intense years with Jesus, just experienced his death and his resurrection. Their grief was deeper than any chasm, and their joy propelled them into the world. They were changed by the story of the gospel so much that they couldn't sit still. They couldn't refrain from repeating their story to anyone who would listen. And they took to the road to tell even the strangers in other lands. The gospel of Jesus is transformative, propelling, and explosive. Because of their work and joy, the world came to know of Jesus the Lord. Because of their work, the outcasts were invited in, and the "incasts" were invited out. Because of their love, the sick were healed and new communities were formed all over the world. Ours is a tradition of great, explosive movements of the good news.

Outside of the norm are the Hopefuls who are watching and not giving up hope. They shake their heads in confusion for what they see, but they do not despair. They are used to the idea of movement and they are already in the unfamiliar ground of religion. In their state of often being called outcasts, misunderstood, unheard, and unfamiliar, they live with great hope. It is not a hope for the church to remain as it is. It is a hope for the church to go into a future of drastic transfiguration for the sake of the gospel. They see it. They imagine it. They know it is coming. And so hope lives on at the edge of religion and religious structures.

THE PATH OF LIFE JOURNEYS THROUGH THE PATH OF DEATH

Choosing life necessitates that something must die—death, then life and more life.

To move from the past to the present and future means determining the way to set aside what worked for our parents and grandparents, and to move toward what will connect for our children and grandchildren. This generation sees reality in terms of mission, relationships, and the incarnation of God on earth.

This church is tenuously riding on its laurels, rapidly growing gray, and is not reaching the new generations of Christ-seekers. Most mainline churches are grasping to find a way to live while watching their own demise. They are seeking, searching, hoping, and praying for life to return to their church home. All the while, they wonder if they should be resigned to the current state of affairs—that their church in their town is facing the prospect of death; that a slow death may be the best they can hope for.

The most difficult factor of death is fear. And churches fear change more than they fear death. It is easier to let things slowly die out with a congregation than to face the fear of death and move toward life. But we are called to life, even life that comes after death. The church in America is experiencing a drastic decline, but we can be sure that, although many things may change, God will make a way for the church to be the church in this present day. The church can go along with God's plan, or she can fight that plan with her last breath.

After the September 11 attack on the United States, Bruce Springsteen's song "My City of Ruins" (which was originally written about his hometown of Asbury Park, New Jersey) took on deep meaning for our country. We watched the fall of the towers in New York, the plane crashing into the Pentagon, and the downed planes on one particular morning. Before that, life was going on as usual. After that we were in crisis mode. But this song spoke of a city facing ruin. The lyrics of this song speak of our current situation in the church as they are, if you replace the word *city* with *church*.

> *There's a blood red circle*
> *on the cold dark ground*
> *and the rain is falling down.*
> *The church door's thrown open*
> *I can hear the organ's song*
> *But the congregation's gone,*
> *My city of ruins*
> *My city of ruins*

Now the sweet bells of mercy
Drift through the evening trees
Young men on the corner
Like scattered leaves,
The boarded up windows,
the empty streets,
While my brother's down on his knees
My city of ruins
My city of ruins

Come on, rise up (repeated 8 times)

Now there's tears on the pillow
Darlin' where we slept,
and you took my heart when you left.
Without your sweet kiss
My soul is lost, my friend
Tell me, how do I begin again?
My city's in ruins
My city's in ruins

Now with these hands,
with these hands, with these hands
with these hands, I pray Lord
With these hands, with these hands
I pray for strength, Lord
With these hands, with these hands,
I pray for faith, Lord
With these hands, with these hands,
I pray for the faith, Lord
With these hands, with these hands,
I pray for the faith, Lord
With these hands, with these hands,
I pray for your love, Lord
With these hands, with these hands,
I pray for your faith, Lord
With these hands,
With these hands,
I pray for the strength, Lord
With these hands,
With these hands,

Come on, rise up
Come on, rise up [44]

The thing I love about this song is that while it sings out a clear problem of loss and ruin, it also points to the possibility of hope. Rising up from the ruins is what we do. It is what Jesus did, and it is what we too are called to as followers of Jesus Christ.

The rising up is happening. I hear about it and I see it regularly. It is happening in dissatisfied pastors and disgusted lay folk. It is happening in the people whom the church isn't yet listening to, the quiet ones who, if we take the time, will tell us about the church they see—the one that doesn't exist on Sunday morning inside a sanctuary. It is happening with the homeless, the young, the ethnic so-called "minority," the struggling poor, the cynics, the addicts, the dropouts. They believe in God's church. It just doesn't look like the one you and I go to. So there is a rising up. It is something Jesus is doing. We call it a Jesus Insurgency, a Church Revolution from The Edge. It is about to rock our church world, and it won't be pretty. But it will be spiritual, powerful, and it will be a fresh move of the Spirit in our midst.

Of course history tells many stories of the church surviving changes, cultural shifts, and new languages. It is certain that, even in this day, the church will survive. But do we want a church that just survives? What is up for question, however, is if the particular community in a particular town, or a particular denominational institution, will have the strength and faith to follow God into the baptismal waters of death and resurrection. We will die. We may already be dead. But in death, the Scriptures call us to answer for the living:

> I call heaven and earth as my witnesses against you right now: I have set life and death, blessing and curse before you. Now choose life—so that you and your descendants will live—by loving the LORD your God, by obeying his voice, and by clinging to him. That's how you will survive and live long on the fertile land the LORD swore to give to your ancestors: to Abraham, Isaac, and Jacob. (Deuteronomy 30:19-20)

The path of life goes hand in hand with the path of death. Don't be afraid. There is a Jesus Insurgency coming.

CHAPTER 2

THE
INSURGENT

RUDY RASMUS

THE INSURGENT

Insurgents are people who oppose authority. They are opposing authority all over the world, and they are very effective. Insurgencies of the past have occurred as armed resistance. But recently we have encountered a new thing: political resistances of the heart that are more effective than the physical, military resisters of the past. But whether of the heart or of the political, all of us have the capability of being insurgents.

The word *insurgent* comes from the Latin *insurgens*, which is the present form of the word *insurgere*, which means "to rise up." If you look at the whole word, it can be broken down as follows:

In + surgere = in rising up[1]

This is understood more easily as "rising up from within." So an insurgent is "a person who rises in forcible opposition to lawful authority, especially a person who engages in armed resistance to a government or to the execution of its laws."[2]

And a denominational insurgent is a person who rises in forcible opposition to institutional church authority and to the execution of its polity.

There is a growing number of denominational insurgents in the United States due in part to the failure of the mainline church in reaching younger audiences, and its failure (its inability) to create new markets. This failure is causing not only landslide departures from church, but an unprecedented switching of faiths. The "U.S. Religious Landscape Survey" details the volatility of American religious life in light of the 44 percent of Americans who have switched religious affiliations or have walked away from church.[3] Alisa Harris of *World* magazine reported that Penguin Book's survey of one thousand UK teens "found that two-thirds don't believe in God—and actually think reality tv is more important."[4]

Harris also reported additional UK teen findings:

- 50 percent have never prayed.
- 16 percent have never been to church.
- 59 percent say religion has had a negative effect on the world.
- 47 percent said organized religion has no place in the world.
- 90 percent believed that they should treat others better than themselves.[5]

George Barna, of Barna Research, surveyed teens in America a couple of years ago and discovered that even though they are more religiously engaged than their UK counterparts, the percentage of young people participating in religious activities drops drastically once they reach their twenties. Could the church in America be on its way to extinction? The appearance of denominational insurgents could counteract this trend if the church would be willing to acknowledge the need for radical change. Beyond the obvious loss of appeal the church has to our younger citizens, the real problem is that the church has so little influence on culture that there doesn't seem to be a desire on the part of younger people to change the church.

There are a number of reasons why religious activities have lost their appeal to the vast majority of current society. One reason for the number of unprecedented departures is that many churches are boring as heck. Tired rituals, bad music, and irrelevant practices compete with 50-inch plasma TVs with high-quality surround sound, multiple brunch options, and an abundance of cozy and richly decorated coffee shops staffed by people who are friendlier than most church folk. That the church is reticent to alter cultic practices that no longer have relevance is at the core of this challenge.

Another reason for the decline is that the church (which once stood at the center of life in most towns and cities) has lost its place of influence. She has become a walled fortress instead of the institution that started many of the hospitals, colleges, universities, and service organizations that our communities rely on today. Could it be that at the very core of the challenge, the church is forgetting the mandate of its founder (Jesus) to not only love your neighbor as you love yourself but also that doing something for the least (in our communities) was the equivalent of doing something for him. An authentic response to the message of Christ requires us to discern the changes that are taking place in our communities for the benefit of those who are blinded by poverty, disenfranchisement, and oppression.

All of us have the capability of being insurgents, but we have some imagining to do. First, imagine the hypothetical situation that the church has been a government of sorts. Let's say the church has been a covertly oppressive regime for sixty or seventy years. The church limits or minimizes access to the system of power for certain people. It marginalizes others, based on, maybe, gender, race, age, or sexual orientation. Maybe it even restricts access for some based on social standing. What we know from looking at the revolutions taking place around the world is that when people get tired enough of not being heard, their opinions not being valued, or the cultural specifics of the institution being out of step with the masses of the public, one has a situation that is ripe for a revolution or a rebellion brought about by the insurgents.

INSURGENT AS LEADER
....

Yes, insurgents will lead the way. They will be young and old, churched and dechurched, and from every hue and social situation. Envision all of these insurgents meeting in the street one day, and saying, "We want change in the church." That may be unrealistic in America, as we are generally a polite society and prefer to throw rocks from around the corner.

But we have seen institutions challenged, like the recent pro-union versus anti-union stands in Wisconsin. One group felt protection within a system. Another group wanted no unions and felt that unions were stifling creativity, efficiency, and budgets.

The United Methodist Church is like a unionized body. Some are given certain protections due to their possessing the union card of ordination, which offers protection to underperforming members of the union. Because they are union members, they often continue to underperform for many years.

Now imagine there is a cry from insurgents, coming out of the shadows, saying, "Why would you keep ineffective, inefficient, undermotivated people in institutions just because they have a union card?" And from the younger generations, "Why do you make it so hard to become a part of the union? Why does it matter? Can't I just come and offer my gifts, and have my contributions be valued in the church?" The answer given is repeatedly no. Any study of recent revolutions around the world reveals the common denominator of the insurgent is youth. Youth who feel the existing system is out of touch with their needs or culture will ultimately respond to disenfranchisement.

Over time, we have created two or three generations of insurgents. They are going to do one of two things: walk away or demand change. They could demand we become the institutions we say we are. Or they could continue to leave. If they continue to leave in record proportions, the fate of the church will be sealed as a once-meaningful institution that forgot to change with time and culture.

INSURGENT AS REBEL

An insurgent is a rebel from within who looks at the constituted and existing authority and structure, usually because he or she lives and breathes within it, and says either yes or no to the prevailing structures. The response is often, "This isn't working for me. This form doesn't make sense anymore." "Rebel" is at the root of insurgency. James Dean, who played the rebel without a cause in the movie by the same name, stated:

Remember:

Life is short, break the rules (they were made to be broken)

Forgive quickly, kiss slowly

Love truly, laugh uncontrollably

And never regret anything that makes you smile.

The clouds are lined with silver and the glass is half full (though the answers won't be found at the bottom)

Don't sweat the small stuff,

You are who you are meant to be,

Dance as if no one's watching,

Love as if it's all you know,

Dream as if you'll live forever,

Live as if you'll die today.[6]

He was called a "rebel without a cause," yet he understood that to live without a purpose was like being dead, and to live without a dream is death, and life without love is empty and shallow. Imagine what happens when love represents true rebellion.

The kind of insurgency I am recommending is the kind that connects love as purpose to the need to change systems in order that more will experience the love.

What attracted me to this faith was the love, not the institution. I didn't read the church's amendments, or its *Discipline* (the book that told me I had to be a part of the system in certain ways). What registered with me was a group of people I met at a United Methodist church who embodied the love that I heard Jesus embodied but had never really experienced in church. I didn't have a clue about doctrine, and as a matter of fact, I didn't care. I still don't have much regard for doctrine that conflicts with the love orthodoxy that Jesus demonstrated. What mattered is that this group of people accepted me for me—without having to know the nuances of my dark past; without checking my economic metrics or my checkbook. They just said, "We want you to be with us." That was pretty revolutionary.

When we think about how love impacts rebellion, how love impacts revolution, we are reminded that this love is at the core of what creates change. Insurgency rises out of the need for change. In fact, the only time the insurgent surfaces is when something needs to be altered in government or institutions. You don't see them pop up when people are at peace or when people are effectively served or treated equitably by governing structures. But let the balance of power slip a bit, when it isn't working, and suddenly there is a knowing that we need to change it.

A close friend once told me, "A conservative is someone who has something to conserve." Think about all the people we identify as conservative. Consider two columns, one being the person and what is it he or she feels the need to conserve, and the other is the why (this person is taking this position). In every case, the person is attempting to conserve power, to maintain his or her position of financial wealth and status in the community, or to conserve his or her name (or traditional place) in the community. But rarely did these conservatives conserve for the needs of others. Really, a conservative is concerned, at least to some degree, about self-interest.

We can apply this approach to religious institutions. Great debate arises around liberal and conservative views. Is it possible that those who could be identified as conservatives are really attempting to hold on to the parts of the institution that give them identity or power?

When we think about whether insurgents will be able to make a difference or not, we are learning from the political and global landscape. We know that when people have need, and the institution is not meeting the need, then that institution is ripe for being overturned.

Insurgents create a new path, even at great danger and personal expense.

Dr. Martin Luther King Jr. believed if you haven't found something worth dying for, you haven't found something worth living for.[7] This path of insurgency is a road worth living and dying for. When we get to the road, we are reminded that the path to change is perilous. It is like a Damascus Road. Or a Jericho Road for the Samaritan. There will be great danger on the path whenever the individual decides he or she is going to be a part of the need for, and catalyst for, change.

And there will be personal expense. I haven't seen anything in life worth changing that didn't have a cost associated with the need for change. I have never seen anything that a person really wanted that was just dropped in the person's lap without effort. It doesn't happen like that. The danger of acquiring the thing that a person cannot live without is the risk of losing oneself for the sake of that thing.

Jesus talked about that thing in terms of the cost of sacrifice. He said there was a treasure buried in a field, but there was a cost associated with getting it. He said that when you are preparing to build something of meaning and worth, there is a cost to the foundation. The great danger is when we pay that cost. Paying the cost does something to our reputation, or to our ability to feed our family, or to the relationships we have established. Those "meaningful" relationships were "meaningful" as long as we were of one accord.

The new path, M. Scott Peck says, is the road less traveled. On that road less traveled, we will find the challenges of (1) loneliness, (2) difficulties that come with being singled out as a troublemaker, and (3) having to do a work designed for a community, only to realize that your only community is the people in the house with you.

Jesus had that moment. He was teaching inside a house, and his family came to get to him. Jesus' family said to him, "Jesus, come out here where your family is!" Jesus said, "My family is here . . . where I am finding meaning and purpose."

You see, there is great danger, for when we signed up to follow Jesus, we signed up for a new path. We signed up to go down a road where we would be persecuted, reviled, mocked, and ridiculed for his sake. Often we don't experience the persecution that comes with following the path because we are not really on the path.

We can think of it in terms of the political theory of autonomy, which is a life of self-rule, in society, but self-determined and often different or even opposite from others in society. Autonomy is the force of opposites that appear different, but may or may not actually be different. But antinomy occurs when we experience the momentum of autonomy. It is the true mutual incompatibility of two forces. Autonomy is truths that look different, but antinomy is truths that are contradictory, that don't touch. The antinomious path says, "This path is right for me or for us, even if it is incompatible with someone else's path." It is agreeing to differ in opinion while honoring the truth that each of our paths offers to the greater good. Many religious institutions are antinomious to culture. Instead of a religion that makes us an island of believers, what would happen if we focused on attracting a world of believers?

The challenge with the path of autonomy is that we often make a determination based on our own personal ideal, and we don't consider the complex diversity of the people around us who should be welcomed on the path. We might think "It's easy for me being on the path with all these people who think and act like me." We even like to create paths for people from other folds, as long as they don't come onto our path. But that's not the purpose of creating a new path. The Jesus Insurgency is creating a path that is wide enough to fit all of humanity, as we follow Jesus together. That's the call.

Where did we ever get the notion that a narrow path, with a narrow gate, is the way? I read the Scriptures too, but was that gate narrow in order to limit and restrict people from being a part? Or was it to help us understand that it will be difficult and lonely? Or that it is a path that one must choose out of their hearts to access? No one can be dragged onto a path and ultimately be expected to walk on it for long. Perhaps that path is not narrow in its exclusive framework, but narrow in its difficulty to walk onto, and in its difficulty in staying on, the path.

Our world would be a pretty sorry place if there weren't people in it willing to say, "This sucks and I'm not going to take it anymore." We would all be part of a chattel system, some servants and some slaves.

God bless the insurgents. God bless the person who is willing to sacrifice her or his own life, health, and safety in order to pursue her or his inalienable right of life, liberty, and the pursuit of happiness, and the one willing to follow Jesus all the way.

INSURGENT AS WOUNDED HERO

Richard Rohr, in *Hope Against Darkness*, states, "In Greek mythology the word innocent (or innocens, 'not wounded yet') is not a complement in that the would-be hero always receives the sacred wounded."[8]

For the insurgent, the wound becomes sacred with (when) she or he trusts God in the midst of suffering. Rohr continues, saying:

> *When the wound happens in a secular society like ours, we usually look for an immediate way to resolve it: playing the victim, mobilizing for vengeance (while sometimes calling it justice), or*

looking for someone to blame, or someone to sue! A sacred culture would never bother with such charades and missed opportunities. . . . Without dignifying the wound, there is no mystery, no greatness, no soul, and surely no Spirit. . . . One always learns one's mystery at the price of one's innocence.[9]

I do not consider myself a hero by any measure, because most of my wounds have been self-inflicted, superficial flesh wounds. But even the flesh wounds hurt. I guess it is just my spin on what the ancient religions called "the inexorable wheel," or the mystery of life and death that keeps turning in spite of my desires to stop and get off occasionally. The challenge with avoiding the wheel means we would remain stuck in infantilized aspects of spiritual development. M. Scott Peck, in *The Road Less Traveled*, hypothesizes that there are four stages of human spiritual development, and I think I have experienced all of them: stage 1 is chaotic, disordered, and reckless; stage 2 is the stage at which a person has blind faith; stage 3 is the stage of scientific skepticism and inquisitiveness; and stage 4 is the stage where an individual starts enjoying the mystery and beauty of nature. Dr. Peck argues that while transitions from stage 1 to stage 2 are clear and decisive, transitions from stage 3 to stage 4 are subtler.[10] I guess I have made a miraculous leap from stage 2 spirituality to stage 4 spirituality. The person in stage 4 no longer accepts things through blind faith, but because of genuine belief is positioned to act as change agent in the world, as a denominational insurgent. That's not to say that I have checked my inquisitive nature at the door of my faith, but it is to say that I now know that one cannot fully experience the mystery and beauty of life without encountering the pain that accompanies the journey.

I was telling a friend the other day that life is like a thrill ride at an amusement park. The paschal mystery or the classic pattern of transformation answers the question for us: "Who am I in God?" My desire is to answer that question before this ride ends and it's time to get off.

A JESUS INSURGENCY . . .

BRINGS JESUS TO THE WORLD

Jesus insurgents focus clearly on the one thing that matters: bringing Jesus to the world. When I think about insurgents focusing clearly on the one thing that matters, that of bringing Jesus to the world, I think, "Jesus was focused too." Jesus was the True Insurgent. Every time people tried to get Jesus, the True Insurgent, off the path, he would remind them that he had to be about his Father's business. In the same way that Jesus was singular in purpose, we can be singular in purpose, and especially singular in matters of critical importance in this kingdom life. We should be focused on that.

In a video interview Walter Brueggemann said, "The great tension of ministry is balancing budgets with the truth."[11]

What often clouds our focus is beginning to think the one thing that matters is keeping the institution alive. In keeping the institution alive, we have a tendency to place priority on a church's fiscal well-being over the spiritual well-being of its participants and its leadership. So, in this great focus on the institution, we are constantly getting sidetracked. If our goal is the Great Commandment, to love God with all our hearts, minds, and strength, and to love our neighbor as we love ourselves, then we get off track!

Jesus gave this charge: "Therefore, go and make disciples of all the nations, baptizing them in the name of the Father and of the Son and of the Holy Spirit, teaching them to obey everything that I've commanded you" (Matthew 28:19-20a).

Never did Jesus say we must focus on the life of our institution, or on doctrinal principles, or on our fiscal priorities. He did say, "I'll build my church on this rock" (Matt. 16:18), but I don't think he implied we are going to do a capital campaign. Instead, "We are going to build a church here with Peter. And with Rudy, and Dottie, and you. And despite what you think about these people, even the gates of hell won't be able to change what I am doing in these churches."

We have to decide what matters. Make a list. If people matter, then we have to determine all the things that matter to people as it relates to this work of Jesus that we are a part of. If buildings matter, then we will have to prioritize by asking ourselves, "What about these buildings matter to the work of Jesus?" If pensions, "What about our pension fund matters to the work of Jesus?" Creating security for professional clergy is an admirable cause. But did Jesus have a pension fund? Did the disciples have nest eggs? No. They took risks in their lives. They stepped out and followed the call of Jesus into the wilderness.

After we finish the list, we will find that the only thing that matters on the list is people. Of course, the first matter of importance is our relationship with God, and also with people. Bringing Jesus to the world is what matters.

When I think about bringing Jesus to the world, I am reminded that we are today bringing Jesus to a world that may have heard of him, but might not know him that well. This changes our efforts around the work of bringing Jesus to them. What we have to do is begin to focus on how we are presenting Jesus because it's for certain that nobody's going to care if they disregard the Messenger.

We have got some work to do. We might have to become a little less judgmental as we bring Jesus to the world. We might have to become a little more loving. We might have to relinquish, for a season, or even forever, our need to control the way people think of our faith experience. We may have to focus on love.

. . . FOCUSES EFFECTIVELY

The global insurgencies taking place right now are many. But on the evening news, all of the insurgents are responding to the same message. The insurgents are not saying, "Let's keep this guy" or "Let's remove him." They are saying the same thing: "Let's move forward!"

We need to spend some time discussing this forward movement. What is the one thing that matters? If it is institutional survival, it is possible that we will survive as an institution. But if we haven't prioritized people, the surviving institution will be a shell with no one in it.

Insurgents have deaf ears for the things that get in their way. Something I've learned along the way is that you really have to be careful what messages you allow to penetrate your ears and heart, because they can affect your ability to respond with passion for your cause. So having deaf ears for the things that get in the way is an essential element because there will always be people who say, "Well, it's all right, so why do you have to go messing things up?" I'm reminded of preachers who attempted to discourage Dr. Martin Luther King in the 1950s and 1960s during the insurgency taking place around racism. A lot of his detractors were clergy who were comfortable in their churches and in their denominational roles. Their words to Dr. King were "Why are you coming making trouble for us? We are doing fine here." Imagine if Dr. King were to allow those conservatives to have an impact on or affect what he believed was his important cause: to overturn a system of racism and apartheid. He turned a deaf ear. And that turning brought an impending risk to his personal safety. Deaf ears sometimes mean we won't hear the sound of the baseball bat flying through the air, aimed at our mission. This means we stand the risk of being blindsided often, and, worse, being hit on the head by the flying bat. But if you haven't committed to your cause to the point where you're ready to experience any discomfort, then maybe insurgency isn't for you.

The interesting thing is that everyone experiences the benefits of the risk the insurgents take. We see that all over the world. In our denominations, there are people standing for the right of the marginalized oppressed, and those people are ostracized and avoided in conference meetings. One day, insurgents will say, "I'm glad I did that because if I hadn't, maybe my son or my daughter wouldn't have had a place to go to church."

Insurgents have strong hearts, and stamina, and do not even care if there are others on the path. They are willing to be alone.

If I could tell my story of ministry, I think it would be titled "Alone." People don't really identify with the radical. We are more a country of followers. Everybody can't lead, but if you really want to be alone in a room, be the person with the opposing view. If you really want to be alone in a room full of clergy, be the one who might be challenging a system of guaranteed appointments.

The role of the insurgent is often seen in big crowds. The beauty of the picture is that insurgents are all demonstrating as though they are alone. That's the true picture of insurgency: a big crowd of people who are there for the same reason but there because of their individual commitment to the cause. The crowd may be shouting and demonstrating and cheering as though no one else is in the group. Each one has decided he or she is there for a purpose. They don't need the crowd, but the crowd-effect draws power in their purpose. Yet, with or without the crowd, they are willing to shout out alone.

If we are not prepared to embrace the challenges of the immediate, we will never experience the benefit of the ultimate. And that is where we are. The immediate will have challenges. The immediate will leave us alone with a few good friends.

NAMING THE INSURGENTS

The insurgents are like the Joan of Arcs, John Wesleys, George Whitefields, and Martin Luther Kings of yesterday. Through history we see that insurgents were left with only "a few good friends." Joan of Arc was on the path alone: a woman in a male military who had a deeply spiritual connection to God, and who was fearless in her willingness to follow God's vision for her life. Based on her era, you might wonder whether she was challenged because she was a woman in the military or because she was hearing from God. However, back then, people were receptive to words and visions from God, so that really wasn't the challenge. Joan of Arc did not allow a patriarchal, male-dominated society to stop her from following her path.

John Wesley was a great orator and a phenomenal entrepreneur. He saw an opportunity to move beyond the Anglican path to a brave new world. Could it be that we are on the Anglican path that John Wesley was originally on, but because of the safety of that Anglican path, we have refused to venture out on the journey and the call that John Wesley ventured out onto? He risked it all for the sake of the call. He had a safe job as an Anglican priest. He had an appointment in the New World, the American Colonies, and he could have kept his job and reported back to the bishop, "All is well," and maintained a little growth, and all probably would have been well.

Wesley preached a sermon on love based on 1 Corinthians 13:3, which says, "If I give away everything that I have and hand over my own body to feel good about what I've done but I don't have love, I receive no benefit whatsoever."

The words that follow show that John Wesley was willing to stand for authenticity and commitment. He said:

> *There is great reason to fear that it [this Scripture] will hereafter be said of most of you who are here present, that this scripture, as well as all those you have heard before, profited you nothing. Some, perhaps, are not serious enough to attend to it; some who do attend, will not believe it; some who do believe it, will yet think it a hard saying, and so forget it as soon as they can; and, of those few who receive it gladly for a time, some, having no root of humility, or self-denial, when persecution ariseth because of the word, will, rather than suffer for it, fall away.*[12]

That is the Word speaking right before you. As a matter of fact, Wesley was willing to say what needed to be said, regardless of how it might have been received by those with influence in his circle.

George Whitefield's relationship with John Wesley was influential. Sometimes we need people to remind us of the essential things in our lives. When Whitefield told Wesley to come and preach for him in the fields, Wesley wasn't excited about the invitation. He had become accustomed to one approach to ministry. Whitefield offered Wesley the opportunity to review his methodology. This reminds us that if we are not the insurgent, maybe we need insurgents to challenge us on our current mode of thinking and doing ministry. We are all recruited into something. Ministry is, at its core, about the request. And when we find ourselves doing ministry one way, at times we need the insurgent to come along and say, "You've got it all wrong." That's it at the core. We have to be open enough in the midst of our aloneness to hear the critique, and even the criticism, for where we might be missing it.

Dr. Martin Luther King Jr., in the same way as Wesley, once said, "Any religion that professes to be concerned with the souls of men and is not concerned with the slums that damn them, the economic conditions that strangle them and the social conditions that cripple them is a dry-as-dust religion."[13]

. . . REFUTES NARCISSISM

The prohibiting factor in the face of effective insurgency in and around the church today is the presence of spiritual narcissism. I vividly remember the day when the church was at the very center of community life. It was a place where people would go for refuge and a symbol that stood as a reminder of the possibility of hope in the midst of suffering. There were selfless, caring people connected to these steeple-topped houses, people like one woman who represented an ethos of compassion. She was also my first encounter with commodity brokerage when she would judiciously distribute government-issued cheese and butter, known in the neighborhood as "commodities," to families needing that extra bit of help between paychecks.

I can't help wondering, when did the church get off track and begin celebrating prosperity as a core ethos, and when did suffering for the sake of others become passé as a guiding principle? Even though there have always been those who have taken advantage of the religious seeker, hoping for a get-rich-quick scheme, with God as an automatic teller machine, rarely in the history of the church has the presence of narcissistic values been more evident.

The term "narcissism" finds its origins in Greek mythology. Narcissus is remembered for having fallen in love with his own reflection. And since he could not obtain the object of his love, he died of sorrow beside the same pool. I'm not implying the church has fatally fallen in love with its own image, but could it be that the church has become so consumed with its own reflection, it has possibly missed seeing the world around it?

In her book *The Narcissism Epidemic*, Dr. Jean Twenge rings a sobering alarm signaling the absence of the historically conscious voice of the religious establishment, which has been replaced with a condescending whisper saying "God wants you to be rich," often offering the notion that it will magically happen without work, investment, or abilities. The few religious establishments thriving today often appeal to our society's narcissistic tendencies with huge doses of individual choices as an effort to remain culturally relevant and open for business. In response, Dr. Twenge says:

> *The religious and volunteer organizations that have aligned themselves with individualistic values have thrived, while those that have not have withered. Neither has played a major role in causing the narcissism epidemic; in fact, most of the time both mitigate it. At the same time, both have adapted to a new culture that favors a focus on self. The religious and volunteer organizations that have succeeded have given the people what they want, which is often self-admiration. . . . It's a bit of narcissistic jujitsu; the promise of having their needs met brings people into an organization, but their individual narcissism is ultimately reduced by the organization.*[14]

I actually think it's the church's attempt to reduce an individual's narcissism that precipitates an individual's eventual departure from the church. After departing church life, the common response toward the religious establishment is often guilt, anger, and rage, accompanied by a lack of humility. Last year The Pew Forum on Religion and Public Life released research that showed 44 percent of the 35,000 respondents left the faith of their childhood for either another religion or none at all.

According to Twenge, the church was once the place that encouraged humility:

> *Originally, religions could enforce narcissism-reducing practices because they didn't have to compete for adherents: if you were born into a religion, you usually stayed. Now, however, people can select the religion that works for them—often the one that offers the most benefits with the least pain. To compete religions have to give people what they want.*[15]

A review of the words associated with Narcissistic Personality Disorder (NPD) include *grandiosity, exaggeration, fantastic thinking, romantic, believes oneself special, unique, requires admiration, entitled, demanding, exploitive, manipulative, lacks empathy, arrogant,* and *haughty*. This provides an interesting revelation. Based on this list, religious people don't have the narcissism market cornered, and all people, both religious and nonreligious, show equal propensity toward narcissistic tendencies. Of course, church folks should at least register a little on the humility survey.

The answer to this dilemma is in judging less, loving more, and facing the fact that "what was once solely a collective exercise has become far more individual."[16] Religion has changed forever. Welcome to the faith of the twenty-first century. Walter Wink puts it this way: "When the church refuses to live out the costly identification with the oppressed it is like saying to the lion and the lamb, 'let us mediate your differences,' and the lion replies, 'sure you can mediate my differences with the lamb after I finish my lunch.'"[17]

INSURGENTS LIVE A NEW WAY . . . THE WAY OF LOVE

Nothing would change in life without an insurgent spirit coming to challenge how we have chosen to live. Life is about insurgency. The key is, How do we mediate our fear knowing that life will change for us? Living in a new way sometimes means changing something.

A man once stood up in a meeting and complained about his job. He was saying that it was a dead-end job, and he was sick of going there. Another man responded, "Brother, what you need to do is start changing your route to work." It was a simple anecdote. What the second man meant was that the complainer needed to change what he could for now. "Right now you can change the scenery you experience on the way to that mundane job." For us, living a new way will mean, at the onset, changing those things we have the power to change. Sometimes we put off the need for change because of the challenge that life conversion presents. Changing the things we can resolve, in a small part, is living in a new way.

Out of the need for a response to narrow, exclusive theologies, denominational insurgency takes on a new way of being. A history of alienation, separation, and stagnation has created a duplicitous kingdom effect of "us versus them," an outgrowth of wanting to control God's acceptance. Anne Lamott states this paradigm succinctly when she said, "You can safely assume that you've created God in your own image, when it turns out that God hates all the same people you do."[18]

The Bible clearly states that we were created in the image of God. If we believe that, then we must assume every aspect of his creation is a replica of God's many facets. It is in the facets of God that faith and belief became distorted due to the human propensity to differentiate between the two. I don't know why we are so quick to draw lines and boxes separating us from one another, but if humans were all purple with big orange polka dots, we would still find a way to critique one another. I do not believe this is God's idea of love.

I am often asked why I am so intense concerning the concept of unconditional love. The real truth comes out of the two hard, lonely years I spent in middle school separated and alone without one friend to eat lunch with, to talk with, to go to recess with, or to ride the bus home with, because I was the only person of a different race on the school's campus of one thousand students. It was at this moment in my life when I became keenly aware of the cruelty associated with hatred and lovelessness. Understanding how cultural isolation felt placed me on a search for meaning that ultimately landed me on a collision course with the answer to isolation through love, which was the faith practiced by Jesus, that became the basis of what we now call Christianity. Interestingly, it was my early encounters with so-called Christianity that helped to delay my entry into organized religion.

I have wondered for years how a faith experience so completely identified with "love" could be associated with so many atrocities of human degradation throughout history. Throughout history, the Christian church has financed conquering conquistadores, accommodated slavery because the enterprise was good for the collection plate, and looked the other way while Hitler eliminated millions of Jews. Does the Christian church still accommodate hatred today because it's good for the collection plate? The sin of silence in the face of any human suffering is the greatest challenge that we face today as followers of Jesus.

Danish philosopher Søren Kierkegaard believed that love was hidden and we only see its outward manifestation. He went on to say in his epic *Works of Love* that "we may struggle to define love in its most concise philosophical terms but we can (only) evaluate the quality of love by its fruit."[19]

If I want to know how you interpret love, I can look to your fruit as a determinant. Peter Gomes said the love Jesus talked about is not preferential love based on a preexisting qualification process, but it is love in the same way that God loves us. Out of this love we are to love "the neighbor" in other human beings.[20] Assuming "the neighbor" is a sociological parameter and not a geographic determination makes everyone on the planet our neighbor, whether we like, agree with, or approve of their life expression or not. If the greatest commandment according to Jesus was to love God (through sacrifice), love others (through service), and to love self (through self-respect), then you had better look and love like God rather than to have God looking and loving like you.

The origin of grace-less concepts of God probably has roots in the human truth development process that begins when we are born, slapped on the behind, handed to strangers, taken home by those same people, who, without a clue, begin informing us what is truth to them. We are then sent on a mission called life to practice the truth we were given until we discover there may be a little more to the story than we were originally told. The devastating effects of this process are compounded when we add in systematically efficient religious theories to the mix, which ultimately become identified as the unquestionable and infallible truth. Mark Twain said it best when he said, "People's beliefs and convictions are in almost every case gotten at second-hand, and without examination."

Before we go deciding that our American religious-doctrine positions should be the ruling force in the world (or in our own neighborhood) we should probably give some consideration to the fact that Wesley, Martin Luther, John Calvin, St. Augustine, and a fourth-century monk named Pelagius—all considered the founders of the American religious experience—were not American. J. Pittman McGehee and Damon J. Thomas, in their book *The Invisible Church*, observe how American religion has become the "unconscious heirs to the ills of our spiritual forefathers" and how the "Protestant ethic is the direct descendent of Puritanism's effect on Western Christianity and American religion": [21]

> Although we tend to act as though the American religion is based in scripture, this pseudo religion is actually only a consensus reality, an outward cultural expression of American ego.

Subsequently,

> the American religion system seeks to maintain the illusion of fairness, which provided the foundation for cause and effect universe. The catchall disclaimer to the law of fairness is that if an undeserving misfortune or catastrophe should occur, no matter how inexplicably unfair, it's because God had a plan.

. . . When this is our response to stuff happening to us, we never take full advantage of the exhilarating opportunity that is always available to us. This is the chance to do what the alchemists could never do: to turn prima material [stuff] into gold.[22]

The new insurgents are taking the stuff that has happened to them through oppression and injustice and are turning misfortune into a movement. A Jesus Insurgency is focused on resolving the stuff that happens rather than believing God is causing it to occur. With this perspective in mind we will begin to realize that stuff is not only happening to us but is also happening to people all over the world, in this country, in our cities, and in our own neighborhoods that serves as a motivation to change the world around us, not just to say its God's will and go back to sleep. An appropriate response from the churches with Jesus' name attached to them in some form or another should be holy disgust and holy rage to the atrocities that accompany economic apartheid and injustice based on societal positioning. And if the church doesn't recognize the need to correct this madness of misrepresentation, there is an insurgency coming to a church near you. During his Nobel Peace Prize acceptance speech on December 10, 1964, Dr. Martin Luther King Jr. provided a framework for resolving issues related to the peril of turning a blind eye to the suffering around us and the responsibility of the church in addressing the holistic needs of people in peril.

Dr. King reminds us that unarmed truth and unconditional love speak to how we should consciously respond to adversity, whether it was passed on, heaped on, or stumbled upon. So stuff has been happening to me for a long time but I am beginning to understand that, as Dr. King said, our reaction to circumstances is more important than the events themselves, and we can choose how we react.[23] And when I begin identifying my situations in relation to others who are also suffering, insurgency begins to swell. The church is ripe for this to occur and an insurgency based on the principles and practices of Jesus can and will turn the tables from institutional survival to a faith demonstration aimed at changing outcomes.

The Swiss psychoanalyst Carl Jung once said, "One of the main functions of mainstream religion is to protect people against direct experience of God." When we snap out of the coma induced by our interaction with mainstream religion and begin responding in unconditional love to people and situations in the manner in which Jesus did, we evolve into other-centered men and women who refuse to drink the religious Kool-Aid as infantilized and dependent subjects of the institutional church. At that moment, we become spokespersons and representatives of Jesus who raised the dead, healed the sick, fed the hungry, restored sight to the blind, repaired the minds of the tormented, spoke with authority to atmospheric conditions, silenced political pundits, challenged religious elitists, and reconciled whores, pimps, hustlers, thieves, beggars, liars, and you and me to a conscious relationship with God. At this moment we become followers on the road of the Jesus Insurgency. Where there is smoke there is fire and where there are Jesus Insurgents there is often a love revolution getting ready to start. Here's a manifesto I would like for you to consider taking to heart, to the streets, and to your church:

The Love Revolution Manifesto

I will not be a part of an institution or religion that judges or marginalizes a person based on race, abilities, gender, orientation, identity, or social status, but I will be a part of a love revolution that fights for the right of people everywhere to love and be loved by God.

Let the love begin.

CHAPTER 3

THE CHURCH REVOLUTION

RUDY RASMUS

Jesus was a revolutionary. . . . If you don't think so, look at how he died. . . .

Our word revolution comes from the Latin, revolucio, meaning,

"An overthrow or repudiation and the thorough replacement of an established government or political system by the people governed." [1]

It also means,

"A radical and pervasive change in society and the social structure, especially one made suddenly and often accompanied by violence." [2]

In a more mechanized understanding, a revolution is one full cycle from an object's point of origin on its axis. When something revolves, it is turning from where it was, completely around, to a different perspective. Whether the revolution is social, institutional, or technological, all revolutions start when people recognize that something needs changing, and that something needs to evolve. So a revolution is a drastic, far-reaching way of thinking or behaving from the norm.

Throughout history we have had social, scientific, techno-logical, and industrial revolutions. We have seen our under-standing of God change in revolutionary ways. We don't see God in the way people in first-century Jerusalem saw God. We see God in light of our technological advancement. Our world is smaller, and we are connected by the Internet and fed by the media. The world is a different place.

When we think of the kinds of revolutions that have taken place, whether political, religious, social, or economic, we sur-mise Jesus. Jesus' presence, mission, and dialogue challenged the core of a society in his day, and it still challenges that core today. In many ways it means there is no business as usual. That's what Jesus' appearance on earth represented: the end of business as usual. This revo-lutionary Jesus is a game-changer. Jesus implemented a revolving of power, structures, and everything that meant normalcy to the people of his day. When we look at Jesus' death, we see that he paid the ultimate price for that revolution. He was attacked and killed by those who ran the institution. His very manner of death showed the depth of his life. On Jesus' cross, every nail, every rock, every drop of spittle, and every mocking word flung Jesus' way was the core need of humankind crying out for a deep change.

If you don't think Jesus was a revolutionary, look at how he died. He was the Revolution. We are ripe for a revolution today. That's the truth. That is our current reality.

THE VIEW FROM THE STREET

As I move around and engage in dialogue with people young and old, I encounter those who don't consider church part of their lives' ritual. When asked, "Why don't you attend church?" the response falls into three categories:

CHURCH IS BORING

....

Many congregations feel that they cannot afford the cost of a magnetic, engaging, exciting, twenty-first-century worship experience. But who said being engaging has fiscal costs? There are few revolutions in human history that were adequately funded. In the case of a magnetic and effective worship experience, the number one element cannot be purchased. The number one element is love.

Over the years, we have asked the diverse gathering of people who have come together weekly at St. John's in downtown Houston why they pass thousands of worship alternatives to attend a church that is, in many cases, miles away from their homes. The number one answer in our periodic surveys has always been "Because I can feel the love." Passion is an element vital to the attractiveness of a worshiping community, and passion is the fuel that promotes change in all revolutions. But do people experience passion when they enter our houses of worship? Or do they encounter systemic institutional boredom born out of the ritual of having always done worship one particular way?

Jaroslav Pelikan stated, "If tradition is the living faith of the dead, then traditionalism is the dead faith of the living."[3]

Traditionalists, by their nature, look to the past for answers for the future. They do things one way because they've always done them that way. I'm not an anarchist (though I've been accused of being one), but my heart breaks when I see churches in our urban centers that aren't touching their communities because they are so inwardly focused, bogged down by their insistence on safety and fear of taking risks.

At the root of the conventional church's mantra of "We have always done it this way" is the term "traditionalism." And at the core of most traditions are rules that separate, alienate, and discriminate. One thesaurus provides some synonyms of "tradition," such as "attitude, belief, birthright, conclusion, convention, . . . customs, . . . habit, . . . institution."[4]

The antonym of "tradition" is "possibility." If tradition connotes the predictable institutional structure with which we have become too familiar, then the antithesis of tradition would have to mean for the church a new attitude, a new birthright, a new conclusion, a new ritual, a new institution, a new set of rules. We will either brace ourselves against the forces of revolution and change or embrace the opportunities that change provides. One thing we can agree upon: the church, like all contemporary institutions, is deeply affected by what is happening in our world.

In the movie *V for Vendetta*, the revolutionary protagonist wears the letter *V* on his outfit. He tells people, "If you are sick of this oppression, meet me at the House of Parliament." One year later, hundreds of thousands of people converged on the House of Parliament wearing identical masks and outfits with the *V* on them. There are too many to shoot. Jesus did the same by imposing his identity on a group of people who bear his name and resemblance of grace. Only Jesus said, "Meet me at the cross."

While the church isn't an oppressor like the antagonist in *V for Vendetta*, it has become routine and irrelevant to many. When a newcomer attends worship, he or she needs a manual to decode and interpret the rituals. The beauty of ritual is lost in the mechanics of ritual. There is great fear and apprehension when someone walks into a gathering for the first time. And, mostly, a newcomer finds it extremely boring. It is safe to venture that what many would-be attendees interpret as the church's reluctance to engage, or boredom, is really a manifestation of the members' fear of becoming attractive to newcomers, which would force a new community upon themselves. In many cases churches don't change because they might become attractive to others unlike themselves. Many churches don't want to grow.

The revolution will combat boredom through the excitement generated in an environment of unconditional love. The one thing that attracted me to Christianity twenty-one years ago was the tangible and practical way Jesus interpreted life and love. He moved among people, all types of people, touching them, listening to them, and connecting with them in the places of their personal pain. That's how they knew he cared.

People heard him interpret the priorities of life in one, simple, two-part statement. He said first, "Love the Lord your God with all your heart, with all your being, with all your strength, and with all your mind." Then he said, "Love your neighbor as yourself" (Luke 10:27).

Truly loving your neighbor as yourself is easy when the neighbor looks, thinks, and acts as you do, but in the days ahead Americans will have an opportunity to love and care for neighbors who will soon fall into the dire conditions of economic distress, poverty, disease, and mental illness. I'm not sure which comes first, the caring or the touching of another's life and circumstances, but both are essential. Try connecting emotionally with others' needs, take the initiative to go to them, to be with them, to see and hear for yourself what their lives are really like beyond the now-deteriorating facade of possessions. When you do, a sense of holy disgust should fill your soul, and you shouldn't be able to stand it until you do something to help. Only then can we fulfill the "ethic of love and responsibility" that accompanies the mandate of Jesus and become an institution worthy of the community's trust.

CHURCH HAS A LACK OF CULTURAL RELEVANCE AND COMMUNITY SIGNIFICANCE

Church and society have experienced widespread amnesia in relation to the role of the church in service to, and revolutionary change in, the community over the ages. The church, which was once at the center of life in most towns and cities, has lost its place of influence. As a result of becoming so heavenly bound that it has become no earthly good, the church has forgotten the mandate of its Revolutionary Founder, who espoused the need to love one's neighbor as one loves self. This is the very core of the challenge facing the conventional church.

The origin for this mind-set of spiritual practices without accompanying deeds evolved out of what Bryant Myers, in *Walking with the Poor*, asserts as the two-tiered approach to the world, "a false dichotomy that separates evangelism as spiritual activity of the church from the social action of the physical realm."[5]

In Matthew 25:24, Jesus melds a physical meeting of needs for the least of these to a spiritual connection when he emphasizes the inseparable nature of spiritual and physical. One of the challenges facing the church today is a result of the separation of the spiritual activity of the church from the material and economic realities of the communities surrounding the church. These realities impact the spiritual, emotional, social, and material empowerment of the inhabitants of that community. Revolutions start when the masses feel left out of the process.

In other words, what's the purpose of the church in the community? And why should it matter whether it remains in the community or not? Robert Linthicum, in *Empowering the Poor*, says the church has three responses that it can give to its community setting at any time.

First, Linthicum says a church can be situated "in a community," when the original inhabitants of the community demand the need for and establish houses of worship in certain neighborhoods, providing worship space to specific demographics. The challenge is what happens over time when demographic shifts occur in those communities and the original inhabitants move or die, changing forever the demographic composition of the church's community context. These institutions often become walled encampments filled with inhabitants who drive in and raise the drawbridge behind them, filling the moat, equipping it with alligators, and daring the new indigenous inhabitants of the surrounding communities to approach the door for attendance. This posture dooms the future to decline, decay, and ultimately disappearance.

Linthicum goes on to say, second, that one well-meaning response to demographic paradigm shifts in communities is to become religious institutions that purpose themselves to the community. These institutions defer revolution by offering themselves as suppliers of basic necessities to their surrounding community, delaying eminent overrun by the new indigenous residents, but resisting offering themselves as homes and places of refuge. The church "to the community" drains the moat, permanently lowers the drawbridge, but keeps the door shut to permanent or inviting access. These churches offer themselves as periodic places of refuge without permanent resident status, delaying revolution for a season . . . but only for a season.

The third response, Linthicum states, is an appropriate response for a church: to become a church "with the community." When a church becomes Christ incarnate, within the framework of a community, the need for revolution dissipates because in that instant the church becomes one with the people and one with the culture of that community. The beauty of becoming one with the people and the culture is what happens when the need for struggle is eliminated. As a result, the house is no longer being divided against itself. Subsequently, the revolution takes place without an announcement or a casualty, and the restoration of vitality resumes. The far-reaching implications give clear meaning to the fact that poverty is not so much the absence of goods as it is the absence of power. And power is the capability to change one's situation. The result of every accomplished revolution is the attainment of power for the previously disempowered.[6]

CHURCH SUFFERS FROM AN INTEGRITY GAP

The third reason people don't attend our churches is due to inconsistencies in the institutional message, or the "integrity gap." My dad always taught me to never trust preachers and church people. He always said, "They are full of shit." At the core of this statement was the experience of a post–Depression era war veteran's view of the inconsistent message of the churchgoer and religious professional, who conveyed "do as I say," but rarely "do as I do." A systemic lack of accountability, a tendency toward self-righteousness, and delusional visions of God-entitled prosperity clocked out my dad at an early age, and millions more over the last three decades.

When the church's expression becomes genuine, then society will sit up and take notice. When we say one thing and do another, our hypocrisy is unattractive, ugly, and our greatest pain. We must stop proclaiming what we don't live. We could easily proclaim less and learn to live up to it. We could pick the one thing that matters—love—and do that one thing well. Then, and only then, will our neighbors be interested in the God of our faith.

Then we will have a revolution.

A REVOLUTION IS DIFFERENT FROM AN INSURGENCY

Is revolution different from insurgency? They are similar. The difference is, an insurgency is an immediate action with a sudden but temporary impact. A revolution is a long-term experience with both a sudden and an eventual impact. In revolutions of political history, some effects are seen immediately in government, and in the life and shape of history. Other revolutions, perhaps the deeper and more lasting ones, show up over time.

Insurgencies sometimes take on negative connotations because they speak to a small group who are unsatisfied with the current state of being. And that could be the case in the church. People who benefit most from the professional life of the church are satisfied. Professional clergy with professional status in mainline American churches are concerned with the possibility of an insurgency—to say nothing of a revolution.

Consider a beach that is eroding. The water line moves a few inches every year, so subtly that the gradually increasing problem fails detection. It is moving, but not like the sudden miles of movement that a tsunami creates. Everyone knows when an obvious disaster such as a tsunami has happened, but professional clergy and people who benefit from the church have failed to recognize the disaster of a constantly eroding church that leaves destruction and despair in its wake.

We have experienced the effect of a tsunami in our churches, but it eroded slowly enough for it to be understood as a "gradual" disaster. The financial issues are overwhelming and immobilizing in the wake of this gradual disaster. We have all the devastation, but because it occurred a little bit at a time, we didn't really experience the devastation. Yet it was there. It's been there for a while. And we are just now beginning to look out and say, "Wow! How are we going to rebuild in the wake of this gradual tsunami?"

There is also the concern that the institution is unaware of the damage. The people who live in the neighborhoods around our churches are aware of the damage because they see the church move back a little every year. But the people inside the building never experience the damage. The people looking at the building think, "Boy, this is terrible." It is a matter of perspective.

What do you do when the perspective is that this is a white, middle-class problem, based on the demographics of the affected populations? The last time I checked, The United Methodist Church is 6 percent African American. It is a problem that the white majority will have to come to grips with. The demographic in America has changed. The latest census data shows the new majority in Houston is Hispanic. In ten states, Hispanics are the majority group for children. Hispanics now account for one in six Americans.[7] So the question is, where are you standing? Do you even notice the church eroding all around you?

ABUSIVE POWER

After years of living on the other side of God, twenty years ago, at the age of thirty-four, I became a Christian. Two years later I became a pastor, making the commitment to live the tenets of the faith Jesus modeled two thousand years earlier.

These tenets include accepting healthy doses of humility, living ethically, practicing mercy, possessing a pure heart, enduring hardship, and making peace with others and self as often as possible. Ethical living is a responsibility of all practitioners of the faith, not in a weird, heavy-handed, autocratic, dictatorial way, but in the way effective leadership moves communities, corporations, and causes forward-movement without casualties. A lack of faithful living among twenty-first-century religious practitioners appears to be the greatest challenge to the future of the church, and is carving a deep scar visible to skeptics, critics, and the future faithful.

My dad wasn't a faith practitioner until he was seventy years old, after walking down the aisle to commit his life to God one Sunday morning during a worship service at St. John's UMC, where I serve with my wife as pastor. I was shocked. As you recall, my dad had always taught me, "Never trust preachers and church folks." He would always say, "They are full of shit." I readily agreed and still agree today. Much of the "shit" that comes from church people and church leaders account for non-churchgoer reasons for not attending church with any regularity. A lot of the behavior too often witnessed or experienced in church and interpreted by the observing public is tantamount to abuse. After generations of this, the consequences are being felt in the pews.

Abusive churches and abusive religious leaders are causing indeterminate and unforeseen departures from religious gatherings and groups, especially among younger demographics in the United States and around the world. Consider this brief but thought-provoking analysis of the challenges of spiritually abusive leaders and churches.:

1. Abusive leaders base their spiritual authority on their position or office rather than on their service to the group. Their style of leadership is authoritarian.
2. Leaders in abusive churches often say one thing but do another. Their words and deeds do not match.

3. They manipulate people by making them feel guilty for not measuring up spiritually. They lay heavy religious loads on people and make no effort to lift those loads. You know you are in an abusive church if the loads just keep getting heavier.
4. Abusive leaders are preoccupied with looking good. They labor to keep up appearances. They stifle any criticism that puts them in a bad light.
5. They seek honorific titles and special privileges that elevate them above the group. They promote a class system with themselves at the top.
6. Their communication is not straight. Their speech becomes especially vague and confusing when they are defending themselves.
7. They major on minor issues to the neglect of the truly important ones. They are conscientious about religious details but neglect God's larger agendas.[8]

Revolutionaries create a new way, moving the church away from abusive power. The new way of the church will create paths of compassion that turn the cart upside down such that the outcast becomes encircled and the insider walks out to the edge on purpose, so that he or she can experience life more fully. The new way of being the church will eliminate the need for, and end the tolerance of, abuses of power. It will upset hierarchical stratifications and replace them with systemic sharing of followership from the bottom up. It will turn away from what is to what can be by the grace of our loving God. The new way of being the church will be revolutionary.

SEASONED RESISTERS TO CHANGE

Once, St. John's was asked to consider expanding its ministry to a possible second location at a church six minutes from our downtown Houston location. Of our nine thousand annual financial contributors, six hundred lived in proximity to the second church. They had given approximately $400,000 in offerings the year before. The proposed second church had approximately seventy-seven people in worship on Sundays, leaving six hundred seats ready and waiting for prospective churchgoers. It seemed like a great fit.

The first meeting with the seventy-seven or so members was a fiasco. I was met with deep sadness on the part of most of those present. Clearly, for them there was more concern over loss of power than for unchurched people finding a place for worship. I spoke that evening of the possibility of growing our membership exponentially, revitalizing the facilities, and developing a significant children's ministry. I even envisioned the potential of reaching forty thousand students at the university next door. The group was nearly in tears (not the good kind) from the thought of change and the impact on their close-knit family environment. There was even concern that some of "those people" we serve in the homeless community in downtown might even find their way to this location. Things took a turn for the worse when one person stepped to the microphone and asked about the terms of the proposed "merger." My reply: "I looked at the next steps more as an acquisition than a merger." Wrong answer! When the vote was tallied there were sixty votes rejecting merger and seventeen votes favoring merger. The naysayer had his say and the letters on their church sign the following week had these words: "Chapel Space for Lease." It was easier for them to rent out their vacant chapel to strangers than to fill the sanctuary with new United Methodists and possible insurgents.

From the revolutionary perspective, those who are committed to change will have to be able to move beyond those who are resistant to it. These people exist in any revolution. They are called Seasoned Resisters to Change. There is always a small minority of people who wields a great deal of influence. They benefit from the status quo.

OVERCOMING RESISTANCE

One of the major factors used by Resisters to justify the lack of change is the financial impact of change. Financial issues for churches hit by the tsunami are overwhelming and immobilizing. The world has changed. Economies have shifted. New billionaires are being created in China and India in record proportions. A revolution has already occurred. It was political, financial, and global, and Paul Revere is just now making it to our neighborhood.

Imagine that you have a checkbook. You have been spending, writing checks, and paying bills for years without ever reconciling your checkbook. One day you wake up and realize that you don't have the same income, or the income you earn isn't worth the same. The church in this moment is waking up to the realization that it no longer has the influence, or the capital, that it once had. Now the church is saying, "Well, what does that mean to us?" We have a huge shift in power that we haven't reconciled.

If the church's interest is in maintaining Methodism, or the mainline church of the 1950s and 1960s, the game is over. But a true revolutionary is never affected by money, because the cause is most important.

Revolutions have always come from a groundswell of people who have been marginalized by systems and processes, and have been excluded from the benefits of the institution. This church revolution of today will be the same. When the rolls are calculated, the people who will drive the next move are people we would count as "professions of the faith." They are people who have been on the outside looking in. They are people who have heard of the benefit of kingdom life, but have never experienced the fruit.

So, on one hand, we have this group on the outside looking in, wondering if the church cares. On the other hand, we have another group on the inside looking up, wondering if institutions and their leaders care. The group on the inside looking up are the members of churches with dwindling congregations who are uncertain about their future and even more uncertain as to whether or not their interests are being represented in the bigger discussion surrounding the future of the church. In this revolution those individuals will become the enfranchised sympathizers. In most effective revolutions, there have been people on the inside with access who have aided the need and the cause of the people on the outside wanting to come in.

This predicament is confronting the local church with what it means to be an inclusive church to the marginalized, the dechurched, and those who have disconnected themselves or have been disconnected through generations of nonparticipation. The burden of the glorious past will make it problematic for congregations to move faithfully into the future, as a result of becoming comfortable with decline. And only through necessity and issues of survival will this discomfort become so unbearable that change will ultimately become an imperative.

THE ANNE RICE EXAMPLE

Those of us who are Christians should notice that best-selling author and novelist Anne Rice "quit being a Christian" in July 2010, according to a post on her Facebook profile. Regardless of what you think of Rice or her declaration, more than 3,600 people liked the statement enough to hit the "like" button on their Facebook profiles. Rice's manifesto stated,

> *I quit being a Christian. In the name of Christ, I refuse to be anti-gay. I refuse to be anti-feminist. I refuse to be anti-artificial birth control. I refuse to be anti-Democrat. I refuse to be anti-secular humanism. I refuse to be anti-science. I refuse to be anti-life. In the name of Christ, I quit Christianity and being a Christian. Amen.*[9]

Rice clarifies her statement as follows:

> *For those who care, and I understand if you don't: Today I quit being a Christian. I'm out. I remain committed to Christ as always but not to being "Christian" or to being part of Christianity. It's simply impossible for me to "belong" to this quarrelsome, hostile, disputatious, and deservedly infamous group. For ten years, I've tried. I've failed. I'm an outsider. My conscience will allow nothing else.*[10]

If all that religion does is identify what we are opposed to, then Rice and I completely agree on the items we both refuse to condemn. Religion is more than a list of don'ts, hates, and oppositions. The power of faith informs us of the possibilities that life has to offer, not a list of prohibitions and pitfalls. Even the atheist icon Christopher Hitchens, in his book *god is not Great*, remarked on the transformative power of "pro" versus "anti" in Dr. Martin Luther King Jr.'s use of religious allegory and metaphor that ignited a faith perspective that encouraged his followers (and faith practitioners alike) to continue pursuing freedom and "in the face of endless provocation and brutality, . . . to become the moral tutors of America and the world beyond its shores."[11]

When we fail to defy xenophobia we crater to the self-righteousness of many on the far right of religious thought. Writer Anne Lamott stated,

> What the right has "appropriated" has nothing to do with God as most of us believers experience God. Their pronouncements about God are based on the great palace lie that this is a Christian country, that they were chosen by God to be his ethical consultants, and that therefore they alone know God's will for us.[12]

It's no wonder the church has been identified as an enemy combatant of society and is subsequently wrestling with catastrophic decline in every quadrant of religious affiliation in this country. Consider this quote from Leonard Pitts:

> Religiosity is trending down sharply in this country. The American Religious Identification Survey, which polled more than 54,000 American adults, found that the percentage who call themselves Christian has fallen by 10 since 1990 (from 86.2 percent to 76 percent) while the percentage of those who claim no religious affiliation has almost doubled (from 8.2 to 15) in the same span.
>
> . . . Small wonder atheist manifestos are doing brisk business at bookstores and Bill Maher's skeptical Religulous finds an appreciative audience in theaters. Organized religion, Christianity in particular, is on the decline, and it has no one to blame but itself: It traded moral authority for political power.[13]

In her parting comment, Anne Rice put in perspective the sentiment of many people I encounter who are critical of the movement called Christianity. Christ didn't fail her, she said. Christianity did. Christianity didn't fail Rice; the people who represent Christianity failed her. The people aspect of Christianity explains why atheist manifestos and books advocating religious elitism are flying off the shelves. Inclusive expectations of religion are difficult for people in search of a utopian religious experience, but the religious practice of Jesus was founded on a transparent and authentic relationship with God, self, and with others that can only be achieved through unconditional love and acceptance. Practicing faith is not easy and never has been. It requires the practitioner to peer into the darkness of uncertainty, believing the best out of people, circumstances, and God, realizing the only thing we can control is how we respond. An authentic response to the message of Christ requires us to return to a novel religious concept with universal implications, and that concept is love, the kind of love Jesus modeled as a love revolutionary. Because of this love we should not only care that Anne Rice quit Christianity but we should also care that anyone would leave because of a loveless experience. Don't quit the movement. Instead, change the perceptions. Try love.

Remembering what is previously stated, this is a revolution of those on the outside who have been historically looking in, and those on the inside who are looking up. They represent the future of conflict and of change that will determine whether or not the church as we know it will exist in the days to come.

REVOLUTIONARY PLACES

One of the dilemmas facing The United Methodist Church—and every other mainline church—is the issue of diversity (or the lack thereof). Every Sunday morning in America people awaken, get dressed, and drive to houses of worship filled mostly with people who look like themselves. Whites end up in rooms filled with other whites and blacks end up in rooms filled with other blacks. Churches with some semblance of diversity are usually churches with a white, male pastor where blacks have crossed the cultural divide, creating diversity. When I travel to other cities, I frequently ask churchgoers of all races this question: "Where is the church in this city with a black pastor and a predominantly white congregation?" I get the same dumbfounded stare everywhere as people rack their brains to envision a post-racial America that has yet to catch up with the claim that America has truly progressed. If the claim of post-racism should manifest anywhere, I believe the church should be the epicenter of this movement, but two thousand years after the founding of Christianity we still awaken, get dressed, and drive to houses of worship filled mostly with people who look like us. More than forty years after the touted Methodist merger, blacks and whites have yet to find each other on Sunday.

I had a spirited discussion the other day with a friend who is white and has been a choir leader at both predominantly black and predominantly white churches throughout his career. He declared that whites do not attend churches led by black pastors because of unfamiliarity with the music, style of worship, inability to interpret the cultural nuances, and the sermonic dialogue. He even remarked on the prejudice he has felt at times in the black church. This claim has validity only until we look across the church landscape to discover that assimilated blacks attend churches with white pastors in spite of the differences with the music, style of worship, and the sermonic dialogue. This assimilation has a lot to do with the fact that blacks and other ethnic minorities in America have made cultural adjustments for centuries for the sake of fitting in, and at 11 A.M. on Sunday, assimilation appears to be a one-way street, with blacks as the occasional traffic.

Robert Jensen, a journalism professor at the University of Texas, feels that the underlying reason for the delayed arrival of true multiculturalism in Western culture is due to the fears of white people. I would contend that fears exist among both blacks and whites in this country. Understanding that Jensen does not speak for all of white humanity and offers only one perspective, his thoughts on the subject of entitlement, privilege, and the distribution of wealth and power focus on the subtle fear of the loss of white centrality and the fears of living in a world where white is no longer the norm. In a recent article in *Yes!* magazine, Jensen states that nonwhite people have long recognized that whites are happy to engage with folks who aren't white as long as the white-centric worldview isn't threatened and that white groups are happy to have nonwhite members as long as the power dynamics don't change.

When we begin to prioritize our humanity over solidarity to our people group and start moving into places where we are uncomfortable, challenging ourselves to seek out relationships that defy race and color boundaries, confronting the systemic fears that create cultures of inferiority and supremacy, we will be one step closer to becoming the church John Wesley envisioned. We could also take a cue from the document that was bold enough to declare in 1776 that

> *when in the Course of human events it becomes necessary for one people to dissolve the political bands which have connected them with another and to assume among the powers of the earth, the separate and equal station to which the Laws of Nature and of Nature's God entitle them, a decent respect to the opinions of mankind requires that they should declare the causes which impel them to the separation.*
>
> *We hold these truths to be self-evident, that all men are created equal, that they are endowed by their Creator with certain unalienable Rights, that among these are Life, Liberty and the pursuit of Happiness.*

The responsibility of deconstructing our tendencies toward separation comes into play when we begin to embrace the revolutionary spirit initiated by Jesus.

IS THE BLACK CHURCH DEAD?

Over the past two years I have been in conversation with Rev. Dr. Fred D. Smith, professor of urban ministry and associate director of the practice of ministry and mission at Wesley Theological Seminary in Washington, D.C., Dr. Smith compiled the following thoughts in response to the role and position of the black church in relation to The United Methodist Church.

As it concerns urban black Methodists in The United Methodist Church, the black church has failed to live up to its historic mission and gospel mandate. With more education, financial resources, and opportunities, we have accomplished far less than our ancestors. Our children shoot each other in the streets, over half do not graduate from high school, and new industries are built on the criminalization of entire generations of our young men and women. We are sicker than ever and are dying younger than any other U.S. demographic. Much of this is in our power to change, with the help of God. Many people in communities where there are black United Methodist churches still do not know Christ. It appears as though we are too timid to share the Christ who has rescued the black community throughout history, and the Christ who has called us to serve.

Many black United Methodist churches are experiencing a spiritual dryness that requires more than renewal, revival, or even reformation. It needs a refreshing of the Spirit of God. The problem is idolatry: the worship of tradition, power, and greed. A love revolution is needed to transform The United Methodist Church into an instrument for the fulfillment of the call of God to serve the "least of these" in the twenty-first century. We need a love revolution to create the Beloved Community.

The Beloved Community

In most cities, black congregations are located in historical urban centers, making ministry in the urban context a critical component to the revolution required to create vital ministry in declining congregations. Urban ministry is the response to a set of complex cultural demographic conditions that requires a specialized set of spiritual gifts. It's not just doing ministry in the urban setting; it is a theological and biblical approach to urban settings and conditions. This is not only true for urban settings, but for all settings that need to transform persons and communities according to the will of God who is Love. What is needed in the wake of the revolution is the creation of a Beloved Community, which according to Josiah Royce is

> *a community where love and justice rule in a community of unique distinct individuals who are loved for who they are in a plurality of their circumstances. Yet, they share a common memory and future. It is a community of interpretation where our stories, context and future hope have meaning and inspire hope and each individual is assured that they are loved.*[14]

The Beloved Community is a community that God has called into being through the life, death, and resurrection of Jesus Christ. It is a community where love and justice govern the daily lives of unique and distinct individuals, where all individual are loved for who they are in their multiple circumstances of their birth, the present condition of their race, gender, sexual orientation, age, nationality, and so on. It is a place where people share a common memory and future as created in the image of God. It is a community of interpretation where our stories, our contexts, and our future hopes have meaning and inspire hope. This hope is grounded in the assurance that each individual is loved unconditionally and forever.

The principles of revolution for a Beloved Community include the social-theological hermeneutic in which all are loved unconditionally, are affirmed, recognize that diversity enriches all, and see hope in individuals' stories.

Overcoming Structural Racism

The goal of the revolution is to overcome the social forces that created the self-limiting social structure that ultimately evolved into systemic structural racism. Structural racism is a form of hegemony that normalizes and legitimizes historical, cultural, institutional, and interpersonal dynamics by routinely giving advantages to whites, while producing cumulative and chronic adverse outcomes for people of color.

In *The Souls of Black Folks*, internalized oppression is characterized as

> *a peculiar sensation, this double consciousness, this sense of always looking at one's self through the eyes of others, of measuring one's soul by the tape of a world that looks on in amused contempt and pity. One ever feels [his/her] two-ness—an American, a Negro; two souls, two thoughts, two unreconciled striving; two warring ideals in one dark body, whose dogged strength alone keeps it from being torn asunder.*[15]

This characterization is especially relevant to the black church in urban communities within a predominantly white denomination, especially in the United States. Constant consciousness of race and power relationships saps strength from many congregations and pastoral leadership, making them ineffective or less effective than they would have been ordinarily because they find it difficult to focus their spiritual energy on what God has called them into being, doing, and becoming.

The Verdict on the Black Church

According to 2010 findings from the Pew Forum on Religion and Public Life, 87 percent of African Americans identify with a religious group and 79 percent say that religion is very important in their lives.[16] Dr. Eddie Glaude Jr., professor of religion at Princeton University, wrote "The Black Church Is Dead," stating, "The idea of this venerable institution as central to black life and as a repository for the social and moral conscience of the nation has all but disappeared."[17] Here's my addendum to Dr. Glaude's declaration: it will be dead for sure if black church leaders don't stop pimping and hustling for personal gain, leaving the communities around their churches in shambles and the people on their pews uninformed, economically crippled, and politically powerless.

Maybe the "Black church" as a historical icon should be laid to rest in our so-called post-racial world, but there are two inherent problems with canceling the "Black church" as a category. The first problem is that there are too many expressions of faith among black people to narrow the category to a Sunday morning cliché. The second is a shortage of whites willing to bravely cross the Sunday morning cultural divide and intentionally affiliate with a church attended predominantly by African Americans. Even though Barack Obama's election win was a profound public testimony to an American desire to see racial progress, I guess we are not quite a post-racial world yet. Institutionally, blacks remain severely disadvantaged. As the National Urban League (NUL) report "The State of Black America 2009" summarized, in spite of an Obama presidency, "African Americans remain twice as likely as whites to be unemployed, three times more likely to live in poverty and more than six times as likely to be incarcerated."[18] Leonard Pitts took to task the post-racial definition, saying, "We have not yet reached the Promised Land and we all have a moral responsibility toward that goal."[19] But before we can fulfill that responsibility, we must learn to speak the same language where race is concerned, and to mean the same things when we do. If the picture of the Promised Land is a church where blacks and whites worship together, then we are still a long way off. We are definitely not post-racial yet.

Dr. Glaude listed the following reasons and explanations for the deteriorating state of affairs in the black church:

1. Black churches have always been complicated spaces. "Our traditional stories about them [the Black church]—as necessarily prophetic and progressive institutions—run up against the reality that all too often black churches and those who pastor them have been and continue to be quite conservative."[20]

2. African American communities are much more differentiated. . . . We are witnessing an increase in the numbers of African Americans attending churches pastored by white pastors. Such a development, as Dr. Jonathan Walton reminded me, conjures up E. Franklin Frazier's important line in *The Negro Church in America*: "In a word, the Negroes have been forced into competition with whites in most areas of social life and their church can no longer serve as a refuge within the American community." And this goes for evangelical worship as well."[21]

3. The routinization of black prophetic witness. . . . Too often the prophetic energies of black churches are represented as something inherent to the institution, and we need only point to past deeds for evidence of this fact. Sentences like, "The black church has always stood for . . ." "The black church was our rock . . ." "Without the black church, we would have not . . ." In each instance, a backward glance defines the content of the church's stance in the present—justifying its continued relevance and authorizing its voice. Its task, because it has become alienated from the moment in which it lives, is to make us venerate and conform to it. But such a church loses it power. Memory becomes its currency. Its soul withers from neglect.[22]

In my experience as a United Methodist pastor over the past twenty years, the plot thickens as a small minority of older, historically United Methodist members empowered by the *Book of Discipline* often determine the fate of local, predominantly black United Methodist churches. Decisions based on the fear of change, reluctance of mixing with different classes and cultures, and the disinclination to share power with a new regime are keeping churches empty, lifeless, and filled with archaic, culturally irrelevant practices. In addition to change recalcitrance, there appears to be reluctance on the part of mainstream leadership to make the difficult call of insisting on new, innovative practices, which could change the fate of the church in question from death to life.

Glaude concludes: "What will be the role of prophetic black churches *on the national stage* under these conditions? Any church as an institution ought to call us to be our best selves— not to be slaves to doctrine or mere puppets for profit."[23] Will we exhaust our prophetic voices, battling issues that have very little to do with the well-being of the people God cares about, or will we offer our voices to the voiceless, hurting masses who have been helped historically by the church Jesus founded. Maybe it's time to bury the black church as we have known it and raise up an ecclesia, a community, a church where black people attend (and so should white people and others) whose members share a perspective of the twenty-first century that prioritizes God's radically inclusive ideas around reforming health care, aiding in rebuilding devastated communities, creating jobs for marginalized workers, improving the conditions of children living in poverty, ensuring no one starves to death, advocating the need for quality and equality in schools in all neighborhoods, and, lastly, loving one another unconditionally.

SEXUAL ORIENTATION INCLUSIVITY OR EXCLUSIVITY? THE GAY ISSUE

Whether a church is predominantly black or white is inconsequential when it comes to the fear and hysteria surrounding the gay issue. The church rule of thumb is still, "We are not going to ask, and you had better not tell us!" And, "We will all sing 'Kumbaya' and pretend that we love one another while actually we are waiting for the opportunity to pounce on your differences." Maybe the church should take a few lessons from government. Now would be a good time for the church to practice what it preaches. Don't bother asking, don't wait for someone to tell you that he or she is gay, just love unconditionally.

Several years ago a considerable number of people left the United Methodist church I pastor in Houston because of my commitment to inclusivity and unconditional love. I refused to marginalize and malign a group of people in our church because they were gay or lesbian. I believe people should be able to attend church without the threat of humiliation, isolation, or discrimination regardless of their race, background, or sexual orientation. It hurt, it was shocking, and I wondered if the church as an institution really embodied the kind of love Jesus demonstrated during his time on earth. Robert Jensen said, "Historically, religions have addressed three key questions: How did the world come to be, what is our fate after death, and how shall we live while here on earth?"[24]

Even though the threat of an uncomfortable eternal residence after death creates a great deal of anxiety, the third question fuels most of the debate that creates division among the followers, devotees, and disciples of most global religions. It's our attempts at answering the question of "How shall we live?" that bring many to draw lines in the sand and to put boxes around what is an appropriate response to faith. How one answers this question subsequently creates impassable barriers between the so-called "righteous" and the presumed "fallen." In light of the human propensity to judge, we are fortunate it wasn't a human decision that called the world into being, even more fortunate a human won't determine where we will ultimately go after we die, and downright lucky that no one person has the answer on how life should be lived while here on earth. Jesus' answer to "What was the greatest commandment?" was to "Love your Lord your God with all your heart, with all your being, and with all your mind. . . . And the second is like it: You must love your neighbor as you love yourself" (Matt. 22:37-38). Deciding to "love my neighbor as myself" lands me often in the cross fire of inclusion and diversity debates. So does that make me too liberal to be your pastor?

Richard Rohr, in *Hope Against Darkness*, believes both the Zealot (the cultural liberal) and the Pharisee (the cultural conservative) miss the power of true spiritual transformation that comes with enlightenment. Rohr says,

> *the way of Simon the '(Liberal) Zealot' wants to "change, fix, control, and reform other people and events." He says the '(Conservative) Pharisee' has . . . conscientized the poor (as to*

83

arouse political consciousness) for the sake of the happily naïve, uninformed, falsely innocent middle class.[25]

The tension between liberals and conservatives on the gay issues boils down to the struggle to determine what is "good." From a religious perspective, being good is determined by one's ability to conform to a set of doctrinal beliefs. From a societal perspective, being good is determined by a majority's definition of normative behavior. Religious folks are quick to categorize what's good and what's bad. Societies rarely agree on the meaning of morality, but I believe being moral in the truest sense means being true to yourself while not doing harm to other humans. In understanding society's need for compliance, Jesus once asked a person, "Why do you call me good?" (Luke 18:19). He went on to say that being good is not determined by obtaining the approval of others, but being good instead evolves out of one's ability to love and respect others. The United Methodist Church continues to struggle with issues surrounding inclusivity, the ordination of same-gender-loving people, and same-sex marriage.

Author and lecturer Tony Campolo said recently, "A biblical model (for marriage) is harder to establish than you think." Campolo quoted his seminary colleague who has identified sixteen models of marriage in the Hebrew Bible, including "polygamy, concubinage, handmaidens, levirate arrangements, purchasing wives, and spouses that accompany political alliances."[26] For the sake of example I have included eight types of marriage found in the pages of the Bible. The Web site Religious Tolerance has provided a helpful article on the types.[27] Here's a summary:

1. "Polygynous Marriage"—Probably the most common form of marriage in the Bible, where a man has more than one wife.
2. "Levirate Marriage"—When a woman was widowed without a son, it became the responsibility of the brother-in-law or a close male relative to take her in and impregnate her. If the resulting child was a son, he would be considered the heir of her

late husband. See Ruth, and the story of Onan
(Genesis 38:6-10).

3. "A man, a woman and her property—a female
slave"—The famous "handmaiden" sketch, as per-
formed by Abraham (Genesis 16:1-6) and Jacob
(Genesis 30:4-5).

4. "A man, one or more wives, and some concubines"—The definition of a concubine varies from
culture to culture, but they tended to be live-in
mistresses. Concubines were tied to their "husband," but had a lower status than a wife. Their
children were not usually heirs, so they were safe
outlets for sex without risking the line of succes-
sion. To see how badly a concubine could be
treated, see the story of the Levite and his concubine (Judges 19:1-30).

5. "A male soldier and a female prisoner of war"—
Women could be taken as booty from a successful
campaign and forced to become wives or concubines. Deuteronomy 21:11-14 describes the process.

6. "A male rapist and his victim"—Deuteronomy
22:28-29 describes how an unmarried woman who
had been raped must marry her attacker.

7. "A male and female slave"—A female slave could
be married to a male slave without consent, pre-
sumably to produce more slaves.

8. Monogamous, heterosexual marriage—What you
might think of as the standard form of marriage,
provided you think of arranged marriages as the
standard. Also remember that interfaith or cross-
ethnic marriages were forbidden for much of biblical history.

One must be careful when selectively quoting the Bible to
prove positions on the same-sex marriage issue. The Bible has
a lot to say about love, but not a lot about marriage as we
understand it in the twenty-first century. So I lean often on
Jesus' priorities in relation to love to inform my understanding on marriage or any other pressing life scenario.

Dr. Anthony B. Pinn, a professor of religious studies at Rice University in Houston, Texas, stated, "Although black churches tend to be socially progressive and have a history of fighting for equal rights, most are theologically conservative."

Being theologically conservative in and of itself is not the problem. The problem ensues when the fundamentalist mindset infantilizes its followers into rendering them normal and everyone else abnormal. Pittman McGehee says, "If we are to create a mature and healthy twenty-first-century spirituality for ourselves, we are called to awaken consciousness and build soul by living the questions and suffering the paradoxes."[28]

WHERE DO WE GO FROM HERE? CHAOS OR COMMUNITY?

Either "chaos" or "community" will occur as the church begins its transformation through a groundswell of revolution. But it won't happen easily, and it won't happen from the center. It will happen on the edge.

In 1968, Dr. Martin Luther King, Jr. authored a book, published by Beacon, the title of which asked a crucial question rooted in social challenges, theological tension, and a climate of change that were not only present in 1968 but are still present today: "Where do we go from here: chaos or community?" Determining where we go from here is the one question that involves answering another question: are we in a post-Christian culture? Many words beginning with "post" have appeared in writings about the church over the last few years: post-Evangelical, post-liberal, postmodern, post-Christendom. "Post" means "after something has occurred," but none of these terms alone indicate what may lie on the road ahead for the church.

King's question:

- implies that we have a collective choice as to how our legacy will be interpreted in years to come, and it will not come without a struggle;

- points to whether we will allow our doctrinal differences to determine our response to the collective suffering around us; and
- involves our choosing either a chaotic state of
  confusion and disorder where no one wins or the
  productive tension derived from community and
  communal living.

Revolutionary moments require us to reflect on our need for interrelatedness, on our inter-connectedness, and our interdependence. This points to our choice of either perpetuating a chaotic state of confusion and disorder where no one wins, or the productive tension derived from communal living based on unconditional love and mutual respect, the kind of mutual respect revolutionaries demonstrate for one another.

We need a church revolution rooted and grounded in love like never before. We really need a love revolution to start in the church, because I believe love has left the room at most churches and has been replaced with self-righteousness and judgment of the worst kind. This revolution of the heart is aimed at engaging people who normally don't attend church because of the perceived hypocrisy in the church and for those who may attend church but see the need to overthrow hostility, bigotry, and all forms of hatred. I think there are many definitions of love, but there is only one experience that resonates with every heart regardless of race, creed, color, orientation, or country of origin, and that's love without conditions.

Loren Mead, founder of the Alban Institute, sums up the current state of the revolution with this:

> We are at the front edges of the greatest transformation of the church that has occurred for 1,600 years. It is by far the greatest change that the church has ever experienced in America; it may eventually make the transformation of the Reformation look like a ripple in a pond.[29]

I say, let the revolution begin now!

CHAPTER 4

FROM THE EDGE

DOTTIE ESCOBEDO-FRANK

CHANGE HAPPENS FROM THE EDGE

Change does not happen from the center. It happens, almost every time, from the edge. The center may hope for and call for change, as was the case with The Call to Action, when The Council of Bishops of The United Methodist Church asked for studies for the revitalization of the denomination. But the output of the studies and The Call to Action are plans in which the bishops gain more power (called "accountability" in the study) and the local churches (the unit already carrying a back-breaking load) are called to carry more, or to count more. This is the problem with the center proposing change: it usually is an external cry that has no internal ability to transform. Those in power in all systems naturally seek to remain in power or to increase their power. It is done intuitively and without forethought.

In order for this Jesus Insurgency to occur, the leaders within *and* the leaders without (those currently on the edge of the system) must be able to make decisions from a new perspective. Church consultant Gil Rendle (citing Ronald Heifetz and Donald Laurie) calls this the "Balcony Perspective."[1] This perspective takes a step away from the center in order to see the broader view. Rendle also comments that we need to protect the voices of creative deviants.[2] So the view must change, and the voices heard must change, and the decision making must follow a new path. Entrepreneur Seth Godin states that new leaders cannot be about sheepwalking, which is "the outcome of hiring people who have been raised to be obedient and giving them brain-dead jobs and enough fear to keep them in line."[3] Instead, Godin calls the future guides "heretics," saying,

> *Heretics are the new leaders. The ones who challenge the status quo, who get out in front of their tribes, who create movements. The marketplace now rewards and embraces the heretics. Suddenly, heretics, troublemakers, and change agents aren't merely thorns in our side—they are the keys to our success.*[4]

Heretic is a charged word for church people. Maybe it is radical enough to get some attention. When a church is stuck on a plateau, sliding in a decline, or not yet recognized as dead, then it is time for a radical dance between pastors and leaders who are yearning to live out their faith in a new way. Since many of our denominations are either discouraged, depressed, exhausted, or dying, then it is time for leaders to lean into the work of the Holy Spirit. This Spirit of God will look different in every place. It will be unique, creative, focused, and filled with joy. It will not be replicable in other locations.

What we know about change is that it comes from the inside only when the inside has been ostracized and moved to the edge (think Martin Luther and John Wesley). We know that the change makers are those who operate from the edges of organizations. They are in, but barely. They are seen as troublemakers, rebels, "not like us," sarcastics, and irreverents. That is why the Jesus Insurgency that is happening right now is happening on the outskirts of religious institutions. (Jesus himself was on the edge of his religious establishment, and from that location, he saved the world.) Institutionaries are not yet noticing this phenomenon as they tend to push away what can bring the very hope they are calling for, out of a need to protect. As Rudy said earlier, conservatives are so labeled because of a need to conserve. The Jesus Insurgency is happening with a mass of dissatisfied church and clergy edge-dwellers who are itching to live out their mission without constraint. They are the ones who are struggling with the reins being continually pulled back, and the loud voice from behind saying, "Whoa, there!" As Jesus call us forward, as the insurgents lead us onward, and as the revolutionaries step into the future, the change process becomes unstoppable.

But that doesn't make it easy, and that doesn't mean it will happen without a stronghold of despair on the past. It will be hard. It will bring pain, even death, and it will come with a price. But it will come. I believe it is already happening, even if one has not yet noticed.

What we must remember from history and from systemic changes of all organizations, time periods, and transformations is that when the edge gains power, it eventually becomes the center. And in time there will be a new edge, and a new force that rises up to be the church in a new way. This process is alive, ongoing, and never ending. It is what the Scripture means when it says, "Look! I'm doing a new thing; now it sprouts up; don't you recognize it? I'm making a way in the desert" (Isaiah 43:19).

God, through Isaiah, is talking to the people of his day. And God is still in the talking business. And God is always in the changing business.

THE CHURCH MUST RELEASE WHAT HOLDS US BACK

The book title *The Tyranny of Dead Ideas*[5] says it all. It represents our tendency to live under the tyranny of the past instead of celebrating the past *while moving forward* toward the future. Churches live in the traditions of the past without even asking God if these traditions are presently getting the good news out. In *Detox: For the Overly Religious*, David Putman states, "Over time we replace our relationship 'with Jesus' with a religion 'about Jesus.'. . . When this happens, detoxing is required."[6]

When the church has become more about religion than about loving God and following Jesus, it is time for a detox, which means the death of what once was. When someone goes through detox she or he can never go back to the drug that persuaded her or him away from real life. The church that needs new life also needs to let some things absolutely, unequivocally, irreversibly die. The drug of choice, whether it be traditionalism, power structures, "factory church," or economic drivers, can never be picked up again. If it is, there is the danger of intoxication or overdose into lethargy. Seth Godin, in Tribes, says, "Religion at its worst reinforces the status quo, often at the expense of our faith."[7]

Religion at its best is supportive[8] but flexible. It provides structure to assist us but is fluid enough to throw out the old and create a new structure when the need arises. Unfortunately, the mainline church has become too structured, like bones that get so calcified they are no longer flexible and break easier. Without the lifeblood of new ideas, new connections, and new flow into the current reality of our world, the bones and the structure of the church become brittle and break. We are calcified. Our religious stubbornness is killing our faithfulness. This is so evident today that it is common to hear people say, "I am spiritual, but not religious." The user profile section on some dating sites has a largely used category called "spiritual but not religious." By choosing it, users mean they see no value in the form or structure of our religious gatherings or our religious rules. They see that God exists. But they do not see that the church is acting like anything but a valley of dead, dry bones. The church is in desperate need of a restart.

Thomas Bandy, in *Coaching Change*, speaks of the need for religious leaders to move away from hierarchical communication and management of a vision. Instead, Bandy calls for giving in to the chaos that occurs during times of transformation. Too many church pastors are managers, who spend all their time attending meetings, focusing on details, and controlling outcomes. Instead, leaders for today will be the ones who attend to the vision and attend to the Holy Spirit, seeking only to follow God's lead.[9] Bandy describes these new leaders in this way:

- Their commitment to moderation reflects their celebration of holistic health, their resistance to work addictions, and their appreciation for personal growth.
- Their commitment to cooperation reflects their readiness to "let go" of control, honor parallel leadership, and empower team.
- Their commitment to poverty reflects their priority for relational over material values, renunciation of economic entitlements, and compassion for the oppressed.
- Their commitment to chastity reflects their single-minded pursuit of God's mission, the simplicity of their lifestyle, and the sincerity of their ministry.
- Their commitment to fidelity reflects their loyalty to their personal, covenanted relationships to spouse and family.[10]

The shift from primary allegiance to the institutional church, to loyalty to loving God, loving neighbor, and loving self is one that is transforming the face of the church. Not only are revolutionary pastors not interested in the structures that have failed the church, they also are focused on finding God's way for being the church today. They are willing to change, and to live into the intuitive knowledge that healthy pastors create healthy environments.

I remember when I went before the Board of Ordained Ministry to be evaluated for ministry in the local church. I was asked this question: "Since you are a young woman with children, how will you be able to manage working seventy to eighty hours a week?"

The clergyman stated that these hours were normal and expected for clergy. I replied that I would not be working that many hours. The gentleman pushed further and said something like, "Well, is your primary commitment to your ordained ministry or to your family?"

I said that God gave me a family and that I made vows to care for that relationship. I did not see a conflict, as my primary relationships with my family were covenantal, just as any relationship I had to the church. I would find a way to manage my time well. There followed a lively discussion about how many hours pastors are expected to work and whether the clergyperson was primarily committed to the call or to the family. The room began to divide according to their stands. This conversation took up much of my time with the board. When did we get to the place where we believed that following God meant deserting our family relationships? And what young people considering ministry today would be even faintly interested if they were told that the work of the church would be all consuming, even to their detriment? And what person who has not yet come to know Jesus Christ would be able to look at a workaholic, stressed-out, lonely pastor and say, "I want to be like her"?

There are things that hold us back: Are we willing to let go of ideas that are dead in order to live again? Are we able to release our firm grip on the *isms* of church life in order to find a fresh way to live? Are we courageous enough to set free what has held us back for generations?

THE CREATIVE CHURCH

THE CHURCH IS LIVING IN A DIFFERENT ERA

But for this change to happen we must first be real about where we are. We are *real*-ly in trouble. We are *real*-ly in need of a Jesus Insurgency. And we are *real*-ly fighting the change. During the previous phase of church innovation, we began to work out of the new thing called "the Industrial Era." The church got organized, streamlined, efficient, and similar. We became Factory Church. With a few exceptions, you could go to any United Methodist church and find comfort in liturgical and musical styles that you experienced in other churches. And even when styles were different, liturgy, robes, and order of worship were similar. In the Factory Church we became really good at counting widgets. The "widgets" we counted were dollars, butts in seats, membership, and programs. We equated making disciples of Jesus Christ with the numbers we counted. The problem was, those widgets continued to decline, and we were not producing a new crop of disciples of Jesus Christ. We have watched our young, the ones we raised in church, *not* choose church as their means of developing faith. We have watched two generations of young adults grow up without church, having no understanding of Scriptures, biblical stories, or faith development. The previous generation is now watching their grandchildren grow up without a connection to God in Jesus Christ, and certainly without a connection to the way of faith in the church.

That is because, even today, we continue to operate out of the Industrial Era. Factory Church no longer works, if it ever did. And I would propose that The United Methodist Call to Action is an Industrial Era response to a dying church. As a church, we have basically ignored the Information Era, and we are mostly unaware that we are now moving into the Creative Era. Much of the church is now two eras behind our neighbors, our culture, and our children.

Holding on with an Industrial Era death grip is our certain demise. When we set ourselves free, and pry our fingers off the need to order the church in a familiar manner, then we will begin to learn the new thing. In order for this to happen, we need to understand how we continue to live as Factory Churches or Factory Denominations.

For example, the use of screens—whether computer screens, iPads, or smart phones—in worship has been a primary change vehicle for innovative churches in the Information Era, and has even set the stage for the Creative Era, as churches realize the visual medium is best used for art, not data. Yet I know of churches in my conference that are still fighting with members about putting up screens in their sanctuaries. Pastors know that screens are the new "pages" of communication. They have talked to their worship teams and their trustees teams, but the people are reluctant, saying, "That's OK for XYZ Church down the road, but we are a different kind of church. . . .We are a 'high' church. Screens won't work in our sacred space."

Imagine if you were a young adult who works on screens all day long, relaxes with screens at night, reads books on a screen, who talks to friends on screens by text and chat, and who communicates at large by screen-driven social media. One day this young person comes to your beautiful sanctuary and the order of worship is written on a piece of paper. He may begin to wonder how old school you are. He may wonder if you care about the earth. He may think a bulletin is a limited document. It is not accessible on his iPhone or smart phone, so the information in the bulletin is worthless, and, in fact, irritating. He jerks his head back and forth, looking down to read and wanting to look up and engage in worship. He gets confused and actually ends up checking out. When we don't utilize the communication language of this generation, we have stifled or stopped the natural communication flow. If the church has a Web site, these people are much more informed, and even more so if the church has a Facebook page and a Twitter feed. But if the Web site looks like it was created in the early 1990s, it speaks volumes about how important this technology is to the church, no matter what information is on it. Some churches are struggling to catch up to the Information Age and are, therefore, still one era behind.

THE RISE OF THE CREATIVE ERA

Leonard Sweet says we are in a transition from "Gutenbergers to Googleys."[11] The Gutenbergs are people who were raised by the book, while the Googleys were people who read the screen. He states, "Most of our churches are museums to modernity."[12]

It is difficult to serve in a time of transition. People naturally demand their comfort zone. To implement communication lines to the Gutenbergers *and* to the Googleys at the same time is a heavy task. When trying to grow forward, and also care for those who have been a part of the church all their lives, the "claity" often get overwhelmed.

Let me give you another example. At the Leadership Summit of The Call to Action, some great things happened. For one, the church used visual, digital technology (the language of culture) to foster a global discussion. That in and of itself was a positive leap forward. Also the church was brave enough to include a question-and-answer session, therefore inviting participation from groups of people gathered all over the world.

But there were a few problems. The look and feel of the experience was old school videography, like a driver's education film or a homebrewed public access show. It felt canned, with mediocre production values. It was not messy enough. The songs sung on camera and in groups were all hymns—no current interpretation of music was modeled. Also, no one bothered to create a Twitter "hashtag" for instant commentary and feedback until one person, unauthorized, started the hashtag conversation on his or her own accord. While groups met in discussion and our comments were turned in to bishops on pieces of paper or e-mails, some of the most interesting, hopeful, and sarcastic comments came from the people of the edge, who tweeted their responses. That conversation was a conversation of deep significance. One theme of the Twitter universe was a holy disgust over a new form of counting, and a new way to develop a class structure of churches. The message was loud and clear: "If churches do these things, and their numbers improve, they will get resources." The other response was a full understanding that bishops would be in charge of counting, and so the structure would continue to be more hierarchical (i.e., industrial).

Even so, I say kudos to those who planned the summit. It was a step in the right direction. Perhaps at the next one, we can move forward in our communication styles, and move forward in the era in which we choose to live. The little things speak volumes, as we all know, and the little things shouted at us that we would continue operating in a bygone era, while calling for a move into the future. This confused message is "crazy making" in a time when clarity is needed.

Sweet describes the world of the former church as "APC Church," which stands for Attractional, Propositional, and Colonial. And he states that we need to move to the "MRI Church" (Missional, Relational, and Incarnational).[13] Michael Frost and Alan Hirsch describe the "Attractional Church" as having a core assumption that

> God cannot really be accessed outside sanctioned church meetings, or, at least, that these meetings are the best place for not-yet-Christians to learn about God. Evangelism therefore is primarily about mobilizing church members to attract unbelievers into church where they can experience God. Rather than being genuine "out-reach," it effectively becomes something more like an "in-drag."[14]

The Reverend Dr. Joseph Daniels Jr. describes the difference of the past and future this way:

> Religious institutions have focused more on self-preservation than on the deliverance of people from the shackles that keep so many of us bound—spiritual shackles, emotional shackles, mental shackles, relational shackles, financial shackles, all kinds of shackles.[15]

Daniels calls on the church to put aside the previous hurts and hypocrisies, and find a way to embody the life of Christ by being a loving and trusting community of faith, where healing happens, where life is restored, and where love lives fully.[16]

Transformation from what was to what will be is hard work. Diana Butler Bass reminds us that most church fights are about this transition from the past to the future.[17] There is a new generation, and it operates differently. This generation sees reality in terms of mission, relationships, and the incarnation of God on earth.

So today the church finds itself right in the middle of the Creative Era. But we haven't noticed the change in scenery. Churches need to pay attention to the world of the arts, including musicians, visual arts, drama, and others. Rory Noland, in his classic book *The Heart of the Artist*, states that, "It used to be that when you wanted to hear great music or experience great art, you went to church. We've come a long way from that, haven't we?"[18]

It is interesting to note that the world of art has been variously connected and disconnected from the church setting. But whether or not the church utilizes the gift of art and music, art and music, along with other creative venues, will continue to be the language of the world. One of the main complaints of the younger generation about the church is that it is boring. "Boring" means these folks do not experience or feel the vibe we are creating. And it will continue to be boring as long as we leave out the world of art in worship and community.

Richard Florida discusses a new phenomenon, which is the rising of a new social class: the Creative Class.[19] This class of people, he states, is thirty-eight million strong and is 30 percent of our nation's workforce. In fact, Florida says they are central to our economy. "Because creativity is the driving force of economic growth, in terms of influence the Creative Class has become the dominant class in society."[20]

The church must take note of this change in our society! If the world is going the way of creativity, then to speak the language of the people will include learning the language of the arts.

Florida further states:

> *The Creative Class has the power, talent and numbers to play a big role in reshaping our world. Its members—in fact all of society— now have the opportunity to turn their introspection and soul-searching into real energy for broader renewal and transformation. History shows that enduring social change occurs not during*

economic boom times, like the 1920's or 1990's, but in periods of
crisis and questioning such as the 1930's—and today.[21]

If the Creative Class is crucial in bringing about renewal and transformation in our day, then surely the church could partner with the artists to bring the gospel to that renewal moment. Art gives us a new look at old images. Art gives value where there was previously deflation. Art brings a new wineskin to the gospel. And deeper than that, art connects to our roots.

One of the ways we describe God is "Creator." Our first writing about God begins at creation where God breathes, speaks, and plays with dirt in order to form the garden, the garden animals, and the gardeners of the earth. This is our root story. God, the Creator, created us. And then God set us free to be artists and creators in God's image. There have been periods of church history that were ripe with artistry, and there have been periods of artistic drought. This is where we find ourselves now: a church community dying for new expressions of the old story; a church community starving for the artists; and a church community unable or unwilling to let go of the Industrial Era numbers game in order to set free the new expression of Jesus Christ in the world. In order for the church to be transformed, it must attend to what God is up to as God transforms the kingdom of God, and let go of what worked in the past. The church, according to Sweet, needs to ask itself this question, "Why is the body of Christ not bursting with creativity, but a bastion of boredom?"[22]

According to Gil Rendle, we are in the time where we need the creative deviants to bring forward the change.[23] Florida agrees, saying, "Creative work in fact is often downright subversive, since it disrupts existing patterns of thought and life."[24]

DISCOVERING THE RIGHT-BRAINED CHURCH

There has been recent growth in our understanding of the brain, and especially the two sides of the brain and how they operate together and separately. *The Master and His Emissary* by Iain McGilchrist[25] describes in great detail how we have changed our understanding of the brain (or two brains—left and right). This growth has influenced our society, especially as we are moving from a left-brain-dominated world to a right-brain-dominated world. Daniel Pink, in *A Whole New Mind*, explains this transition:

> Today, the defining skills of the previous era—the "left brain" capabilities that powered the Information Age—are necessary but no longer sufficient. And the capabilities we once disdained or thought frivolous—the "right-brain" qualities of inventiveness, empathy, joyfulness, and meaning—increasingly will determine who flourishes and who flounders. For individuals, families, and organizations, professional success and personal fulfillment now require a whole new mind.[26]

Pink describes that we have lived in a world that has emphasized and rewarded the left-brain dominance. The left hemisphere,

> sequential, literal, functional, textual, and analytic, Ascendant in the Information Age, exemplified by computer programmers, prized by hardheaded organizations, and emphasized in schools, this approach is directed by left-brain attributes, toward left-brain results.[27]

Our most recent cultural past has been focused on left-brain dominance. But things are quickly changing and the new dominance is right-brained. "Instead, the R-Directed aptitudes so often disdained and dismissed—artistry, empathy, taking the long view, pursuing the transcendent—will increasingly determine who soars and who stumbles. It's a dizzying—but ultimately inspiring change."[28]

According to Michael Mauboussin, the prominent mistake we make is "a tendency to favor the inside view over the outside view. An inside view considers a problem by focusing on the specific task and by using information that is close at hand, and makes predictions based on that narrow and unique set of inputs."[29]

Mauboussin recognizes that the change must come from the edge:

*The outside view asks if there are similar situations that can pro-
vide a statistical basis for making a decision. Rather than seeing a
problem as unique, the outside view wants to know if others have
faced comparable problems and, if so, what happened. The outside
view is an unnatural way to think, precisely because it forces people to set aside all the cherished information they have gathered.*[30]

The inside view is full of blinders of optimism and even,
Mauboussin says, of superiority and control. The outsider
view is full of questions, seeking new phenomena, and of
unknown possibilities.[31]

What does it mean for the church to live into the Era of
Creativity and into right-brained thinking? It means we no
longer focus on numbers, but on relationships and connections. It means we shy away from structures that demand
more of its adherents and move to structures that support and
set free its teammates. It means we change the course of ritual
to creative expression. For some religious structures, this
move could mean that the very structure itself has to lay down
all it has been in order to live into the future. It may mean that
strategic boldness becomes the norm, and hiding behind the
rules becomes the cowardly thing to do.

A right-brained denomination is willing to let the structure
take a backseat so that risky, creative ventures can rise up out
of the ashes. The backseat is a great place to encourage and lift
up the times when creative souls risk forward, even when the
risking is seemingly a failure. The backseat is a good place to
look out at the horizon and see what is coming, and encourage drivers with future hopes and realities. The backseat,
however, is not a place to nag or demand. It is, rather, a place
to vision forward.

Denominational systems are calling for change. But they
must call in a creative, inviting, joy-filled, liberating, relational
manner. Otherwise their calls will not be heard. Say a church
wants to take its worship out to a place where society gathers,
so the leaders decide to rent out the current building to a pri-
vate school at a hefty price. That price is then enough to fund
the new mission setting. So the church finds a place that is
open in a popularly used commercial center. This center

already has a coffee shop, a sandwich shop, and a grocery store. The church leaders hope to add value to this commercial corner with a church that meshes with the vendors. It is not the intent of the church to eventually take over this corner property, but to live in the locations where society already meets.

In order for this change of venue to happen, the church must go through many layers of approval within the denomination, as well as the church body itself. The process for approvals becomes so cumbersome that it brings discouragement and dissension within the body. Eventually, the church wears down, and sets its plans for a move into the community on the shelf.

If the denominational structure could set the systemic bars lower so that change can be streamlined, then it would be acting as a right-brained, creative system. The denomination could choose to suspend some rules while calling for creative moves, and support risky behaviors even when—no, *especially* when—they fail. Creative people and creative systems require structural support and foundational faithfulness.

CREATIVITY CAN MAKE THE CHANGE HAPPEN

The new trend in churches is toward small gatherings. Seth Godin titled one of his books *Small Is the New Big*.[32] In part, large churches have grown because of their focus on small groups. In the world of megachurches, both small and large have the possibility for growth. But the real excitement is that truly small churches can find strength to change and become vibrant communities of faith. Godin states:

> The first thing a leader can focus on is the act of tightening the tribe. It's tempting to make the tribe bigger, to get more members, to spread the word. This pales, however, when juxtaposed with the effects of a tighter tribe. A tribe that communicates more quickly, with alacrity and emotion, is a tribe that thrives.[33]

Communities of faith can tighten up by focusing on developing a community that makes disciples of Jesus Christ. It may seem counterintuitive to grow small first, but it is the way that Jesus operated. He focused all his leadership on a dozen-plus individuals, who in turn changed the world. When our churches stop focusing on statistics, buildings, and rote memory, and when our churches begin to dig deep into the faith of their fathers and mothers and provide faith-support for seekers, then the church will reverse its decline of influence in the world.

In *The Rise of the Creative Class*, Florida shows an example of a community that chose to be creative. The city of Memphis took on the challenge of creating a new way of living into their future by writing a manifesto. "The Memphis Manifesto" includes these principles:

1. Cultivate and reward creativity.
2. Invest in the creative exosystem.
3. Embrace diversity.
4. Nurture the creatives.
5. Value risk-taking.
6. Be authentic.
7. Invest in and build on quality of place.
8. Remove barriers to creativity, such as mediocrity, intolerance, disconnectedness.
9. Take responsibility for change in your community. Improvise.
10. Ensure that every person, especially children, has the right to creativity.[34]

The manifesto ends with this declaration: "We accept the responsibility to be the stewards of creativity in our communities. We understand the ideas and principles in this document may be adapted to reflect our community's unique needs and assets."[35]

There is today a clear and consistent call to be the Creative Church, to live into the love of our Creator God. The call is full of surprise, delight, wonder, and beauty. And the way forward will bring us to encounter the Greatest Artist of All Time.

THE MAVERICK FUTURE CHURCH

Consider "mavericks." William Taylor and Polly LaBarre studied companies that are considered mavericks. They found that these companies are sure in their purpose and "each company's strategy tends to be as edgy as it is enduring, as disruptive as it is distinctive, as timely as it is timeless."[36]

Maverick companies choose to go a different route, knowing that risk is part of growth, and failure part of success. Mavericks dare to be genuine, even when "genuine" means you call yourself a "sarcastic Lutheran," and wear tattoos without apology, as does Rev. Nadia Bolz-Weber.[37] Mavericks are also willing to look outside of the company for ideas and problem solving. They state that going to the outside for solutions is a regular aspect of becoming innovative in nature.[38] They are even willing to open source their problems.

Maverick churches could learn from this study. If we chose to be willing to go to the edge to find the places where Christ is calling us; if we allowed ourselves to be disruptive instead of perfect; and if we found ways to work as if the day of the Lord was coming soon, then our passion for proclamation of the good news to all God's people would rise above our reluctance to stir the waters of our religious systems, our pension systems, and our retirement accounts. To be a maverick church means to be willing to look outside our boxes and follow Christ down a new, unknown, mysterious, and miraculous path.

The business world also looks at behaviors that can turn around systems. Jim Collins says, "If you want to reverse decline, be rigorous about what not to do."[39]

Paying attention to behaviors that are detrimental to change is important if the church wants to be transformed. Oftentimes, ingrained behaviors are so automatic that churches don't see how they are creating damage. Choosing to do things that bring health, and stopping behaviors that bring disease, can be transformative. Bringing in a new person, and hearing his or her experience of your setting and community, is a way to find out what behaviors are detrimental. Churches can learn to let some things die on purpose, so that life can be sustained.

ONWARD CHRISTIAN CHURCH

Howard Schultz tells the story of the rise and then downward turn of Starbucks. He says that along the way it became driven by the metric of economics (making money) and forgot its original measure that a perfect shot of espresso provides personal connection.[40] He states, "the Starbucks Experience— personal connection—is an affordable necessity. We are all hungry for community."[41]

Schultz had taken the company to its heights, and then took a step back and gave up his position as CEO. He became, instead, chairman and chief global strategist. In these roles, he lost the ability to be involved in the day-to-day operations and decisions. I would say he moved to the edge of his own company. As things changed, Schultz intuited that the soul of his company was being lost, and that the economic rise seemed to be all that mattered. Over time, this loss of focus caused a downturn in profits. Schultz decided to lead his company as CEO again. He states, "Companies pay a price when their leaders ignore things that may be fracturing their foundation. Starbucks was no different."[42]

Schultz could see that the company was failing because it forgot its original love. And in store after store, the customer connection, the coffee experience, and the joy were being lost. He made a radical decision to close down all the stores on the same day and retrain the staff on the core value of making a beautiful espresso, of connecting with customers, and of becoming a community around excellent coffee. He had to let some things go. He set aside the driving metric of making money and forced economics to take a backseat to the original dream.

Starbucks went forward with a plan that looked like this,

> *First, Starbucks had to improve the current state of its US retail business. . . . To do that, we would immediately slow the rapid-fire pace of new store openings. We would also evaluate and then close underperforming locations. . . .*
>
> *Second . . ., we would reignite the emotional attachment with customers.*
>
> *Third, we would immediately begin to make long-term changes to the foundation of our business. . . . The only sacred cows, the two elements I'd refuse to strip from the company no matter how much others pushed me, were our employee health-care program and the quality of our coffee.*[43]

Lastly, Schultz remembered that the best beans, the ones used in the Starbucks experience, were the arabica beans. These beans "grow under some degree of stress, like high altitudes, intense heat, or long dry periods. Such harsh weather conditions can produce high-quality beans, but also fewer beans per tree."[44]

The story has much to say to the current state of our church. There are leaders from within who have taken a seat on the edge. They are there because they were pushed aside, are fed up, have a great love, and they know the edge can be a place of change or a place to bail. Both options are tempting. These Revolutionary Edgers are the ones who can speak into our current situation and bring hope again. If heard and valued, they are the ones who will lead us. They are mostly young, although some are in retirement; they are racially diverse; they are in small, forgotten churches and large, noticed churches; they are in positions without power; they are in all strata of the organism of the church, but operating both overtly within and covertly without. If we let them in, we may be surprised by their passion, wisdom, and vision.

The church has lost its original focus. John Wesley did many things well, but two were of great importance: he took the gospel out of the church buildings and into the streets (where he shared the gospel story and cared for the poor, outcasts, and forgotten ones), and he formulated a way for people to grow as followers of Jesus Christ in community with fellow followers (by asking the question, "How goes it with your soul?"). Of course, Wesley did many other things well: he called for a passionate worship utilizing the current sounds and instruments of popular society; he sent out laypersons to become pastors; he gathered the clergy annually to care for their needs and to engage in holy conferencing; and he gave away what he began to Francis Asbury and Thomas Coke, recognizing that they were the new leaders of their day.

Yet today Wesley's spiritual descendants are engaged in ritual, committee work, membership antics, and fund-raising. In many ways, the greater church has lost its focus. And it is time to get it back. Its time to become spiritual but not so religious. It is time to work with the poor and the hurting of our day. It is time to make grown-up disciples, not baby pew-sitters. It is time to get out of the building again, and hit the streets with the message of hope for a world dying to hear it. It is time.

Church leaders need to take hold of the reins again. We clergy need to remember the command at our ordination, "Take thou authority!" This charge does not give us the luxury of sitting back on our pension plans and groaning about the problems of our current situation. This charge calls us to look well at what is going on . . . to take a balcony view, and then to get out and change our part of the problem. We all can do something miraculous at the crossroad of our ministry. We have a voice. We have a small, and sometimes large, following. We have the greatest power tool ever: we have the love of Jesus. That's really all we need. Really, that's the "program," that's the "accounting," that's the "mission," that's the "economy," and that's the "way to grow up disciples." It's that simple. Take one step forward . . . and follow God's desire.

And we can take notes from the CEO of Starbucks and follow a few methodical steps:

1. We can give special attention to the U.S. church's transformation. We might have to close some churches, and we might have to slow the pace of our best-laid plans, but the church in America is on life support, and may even be dead as we know it. Now is the time to make room for God to breathe life into our dry bones. We can find our center again, and then stick to it. We must pay attention, listen, and change.
2. We need to become passionately in love with people. All people. Not just the people who look like us or believe like us. We need to fall desperately in love with the people and the world that Jesus died for. Jesus didn't die for the church. He died for the world. For God so loved the world. . . . Church, and church structures, must resemble that described in Galatians 5: entities where the fruit of "love, joy, peace, patience, kindness, goodness, faithfulness, gentleness, and self–control" (vv. 22-23) are the markers of our fruitfulness, and the only accounting known to the world. We must love again.
3. We must "immediately begin to make long-term changes to the foundation" of our church. Our foundation is crumbling, but not the God of our foundation. God is merely calling us to a new thing in this day. We must choose our sacred cows wisely . . . letting all else fall away. It is hard to turn around a large ship, but it is not impossible. With God, remember, nothing is impossible.

Of course we who follow Christ know that when life gets difficult, we come out better in the end. We remember how the blind man saw light, and the lame man walked. We know that Lazarus was stinking to death and he walked out of his tomb. We know that what is crushed makes new wine, that what is beaten covers our sins, and what was mocked brings pure love. We serve a Savior who was crucified on a cross, *and then rose!* Death itself couldn't hold back Love. We are the people of the cross, and so yes, we know that beauty comes out of stress and hardship.

The church has died and risen before. It's just that you and I thought we would be following God in a time of living. Instead, we are being faithful in a time of *dying*. But when we give in to death, then the Jesus Insurgency begins, and then we are able to rise up to God's way.

It is Saturday night, and the family has all gone to bed as I finish this chapter. I hope there is some good that comes out of the discussions that we must be having in the church right now, and I know these thoughts, Rudy's and mine, are only a small part of the conversation. But I am thinking about tomorrow—about giving a sermon on a very special day. It seems fitting that I conclude this writing on this night. For tomorrow is Easter Sunday. Tomorrow we know God conquered our greatest fears and heard our deepest hope. Tomorrow we know that nothing can stop God, not even death. Tomorrow we know that joy comes in the morning. My hope tonight is that God will show the way for insurgents, revolutionaries, sarcastics, outcasts, incasts, institutionaries, guards, edgers, and those who haven't yet heard the news—the good news. My deepest hope is that we follow Jesus. For he has risen! He has risen indeed.

POSTSCRIPT

N. T. Wright reminds us of the ancient understanding of what was known as "a fresh grasp of the Celtic tradition of 'thin places,' places where the curtain between heaven and earth seems almost transparent."[45]

The "thin places" exist in the local places where the church is thriving, following Jesus, and filled with joy. They exist despite their experiences of death. They are rising up to follow Jesus into the world. For sometimes we *do* see heaven on earth. In Houston there is a church that went from near-dead to a risen, vibrant, loving community. There the gospel is heard in preaching, in music, and in intense work with the poor and homeless. Pastor Rudy has been privileged to see a bit of life in the Love Revolution. It hasn't been easy, but it has been very good.

In Phoenix, there is a church that is rising up from the place of great difficulty and long suffering. I (Dottie) have been delighted to watch life rising in a church that feeds the hungry, worships with passion, and has changed from an elderly Anglo community to become a younger, multicultural, and multi-socioeconomic congregation. Though we have a long way to grow, this is heaven touching earth. And, by the way, Easter was fabulous!

Rudy and I have been witnesses to the Jesus Insurgency. It is happening on the edge, and soon it will be spreading across the church. For God will bring to us all the experience of the "thin places," where heaven touches earth and Jesus is lifted up. Perhaps then we'll be able to live out the poem of Langston Hughes,

I've been scarred and battered. . . .

I'm still here![46]

NOTES

1. AT THE CROSSROADS

1. The United Methodist Church Operational Assessment Project, Executive Summary Presentation. Prepared by APEX HG LLC, June 29, 2010; 182, 183.

2. According to General Council on Finance and Administration of The United Methodist Church.

3. George Barna and Tony and Felicity Dale, *The Rabbit and the Elephant* (Carol Stream, Ill.: Tyndale House Foundation, 2009), 148.

4. John Dart, *Christian Century*, Nov. 29, 2003. http://findarticles.com/p/articles/mi_m24_120/ai_111531665/ (accessed May 5, 2010).

5. Huffpost Religion. *The World Is Their Parish: Can The United Methodist Church Survive?* By Kelly Figueroa-Ray. Posted 04/2/11. http://www.huffingtonpost.com/kelly-figueroaray/the-world-is-their-parish.com (accessed 4/11/11).

6. See http://www.awfumc.org/pages/detail/361

7. See more of this story at http://www.kpho.com/community/20150356/detail.html.

8. O'Keefe, www.ginkworld.net, http://ginkworld.net/?s=your+church+sucks&task=search (accessed August 5, 2009).

9. William C. Taylor and Polly Labarre, *Mavericks at Work* (New York: HarperCollins Publishers, 2006), 35.

10. David B. Barrett, *World Christian Encyclopedia* (Oxford University Press, 2001).

11. Luke Timothy Johnson, *Among the Gentiles, Greco-Roman Religion and Christianity* (London: Yale University Press, 2009), 282.

12. Ibid.

13. Rich Peck, "Call to Action Seeks Revitalization," *United Methodist News Service*, April 19, 2010. http://www.umportal.org/article.asp?id=6649

14. Scott J. Jones and Bruce R. Ough, *The Future of The United Methodist Church, 7 Vision Pathways* (Nashville: Abingdon Press, 2010), xxi.

15. *Book of Discipline of The United Methodist Church*, 2008 (Nashville: Abingdon, 2008), 87.

16. UMC Call to Action: Vital Congregations Research Project, Findings Report for Steering Team, June 28, 2010. Towers Watson. http://www.umc.org/atf/cf/%7Bdb6a45e4-c446-4248-82c8-e131b6424741%7D/CV_PRE-SENTATION.PDF.

17. "Willow Creek Reveal Study—a Summary" The Christian Coaching Center. By Russ Rainey, PhD http://www.christiancoachingcenter.org/index.php/russ-rainey/coachingchurch2/ (accessed April 11, 2011).

18. *The United Methodist Operational Assessment Project, Executive Summary Presentation*, Prepared by APEX HG LLC, June 29, 2010, 25.

19. Ibid.

20. Ibid., 1–2 of Appendix A

21. Ibid., 172, 24 of *Mission, Values and Cultural Findings*.

22. Ibid., 23, 171.

23. I would encourage every United Methodist clergy, lay leader, and any other leader or persons passionate about the church, to read *The United Methodist Church Operational Assessment Project Executive Summary Presentation*, found at http://www.umc.org/site/c.lwL4KnN1LtH/b.5792195/k.BDBE/Call_to_Action_Reordering_the_Life_of_the_Church.htm. And I would encourage leadership across Mainline denominations to also read this study and learn from our mistakes, and our current state of affairs. This study was in-depth and costly, and perhaps other denominational leaders can take our failings and find building blocks for change within their own body of Christ.

24. Randy L. Maddox, ed., *Rethinking Wesley's Theology* (Nashville: Abingdon Press, 1998), 32.

25. Heather Hahn, "Reclaiming lay leadership key to revival." *A UMNS Report*, July 29, 2010. http://www.umc.org/site/apps/nlnet/content3.Aspx?c=1wL4KnN.

26. Eugene H. Peterson, *A Long Obedience in the Same Direction, Discipleship in an Instant Society* (Downer's Grove, Ill.: InterVarsityPress, 2000), 31.

27. Pip Coburn, *The Change Function: Why Some Technologies Take Off and Others Crash and Burn* (Portfolio, 2006), 19–20.

28. Andrew Root, *The Promise of Despair*, 74.

29. Ibid., 75.

30. Robert E. Quinn, *Deep Change*, 18.

31. Ibid., 18–24.

32. Ibid., 66.

33. *Disputation of Doctor Martin Luther on the Power and Efficacy of Indulgences*, by Dr. Martin Luther (1517). Published in Works of Martin Luther, trans. and ed. Adolph Spaeth; L. D. Reed; Henry Eyster Jacobs; et al. (Philadelphia: A. J. Holman Company, 1915), Vol. 1, 29–38.

34. Ibid. http://www.iclnet.org/pub/resources/text/wittenberg/luther/web/ninetyfive.html.

35. Clay Shirkey, *Here Comes Everybody* (New York: Penguin Books, 2008), 55–78.

36. Stephen Tomkins, *John Wesley: A Biography* (Oxford, England: Lion Publishing, 2003).

37. *Sacred Destinations, sacred places/religious art.* Bunhill Fields, London. http://www.sacred-destinations.com/england/london-bunhill-fields, accessed April 16, 2011.

38. Ibid.

39. Dwight J. Friesen, *Thy Kingdom Connected* (Grand Rapids: Baker Books, 2009), 97.

40. Leonard Sweet, *Nudge: Awakening Each Other to the God Who's Already There* (Colorado Springs: David C. Cook. 2010), 16.

41. Ibid., 27.

42. Ibid.

43. Andrew Walls and Cathy Ross, eds., *Mission in the 21st Century: Exploring the Five Marks of Global Mission* (Maryknoll, N.Y.: Orbis Books, 2008), 10.

44. "My City Of Ruins" by Bruce Springsteen. Copyright © 2001 Bruce Springsteen (ASCAP). Reprinted by permission. International copyright secured. All rights reserved.

2. THE INSURGENT

1. http://www.etymonline.com/index.php?term=insurgent.

2. Dictionary.com http://dictionary.reference.com/browse/insurgent.

3. Pew Forum on Religion and Public Life, "U.S. Religious Landscape Survey," http://religions.pewforum.org/ (accessed July 26, 2011).

4. Alisa Harris, "UK teens: Reality TV outranks religion," http://online.worldmag.com/2009/06/22/uk-teens-reality-tv-outranks-religion/ (accessed June 22, 2009).

5. Ibid.

6. http://www.goodreads.com/author/quotes/1505445.James_Dean.

7. Clayborne Carson, ed., *The Autobiography of Martin Luther King, Jr.* (New York: Grand Central Publishing, 2001).

8. Richard Rohr, *Hope against Darkness: The Transforming Vision of Saint Francis in an Age of Anxiety* (Cincinnati: St. Anthony Messenger Press, 2001), 55.

9. Ibid., 56.

10. M. Scott Peck, *The Road Less Traveled: A New Psychology of Love, Traditional Values and Spiritual Growth* (New York: Touchstone, 1988), 18.

11. Quote was taken from a video interview featuring Dr. Walter Bruggemann produced by First United Methodist Church, Winter Park, Fl for the Passionate Leadership Conference 2011.

12. John Wesley, "On Love (Sermon 139)," – ed. Thomas Jackson, http://new.gbgm-umc.org/umhistory/wesley/sermons/139/. Preached at Savannah, February 20, 1736.

13. Martin Luther King Jr., *Stride Toward Freedom* (Boston: Beacon Press, 1979), 36.

14. Jean Twenge and W. Keith Campbell, *The Narcissism Epidemic* (New York: Free Press, 2009), 330.

15. Ibid., 332.

16. Ibid., 339.

17. Walter Wink, *Jesus and Nonviolence: A Third Way* (Minneapolis: Fortress Press, 2003), 4.

18. Anne Lamott, *Bird by Bird: Some Instructions on Writing and Life* (New York: Pantheon, 1994), 22.

19. Søren Kierkegaard, *Works of Love*, Hong Translation (New York: Harper Torchback, 1962)

20. Peter Gomes, *The Scandalous Gospel of Jesus* (New York: Harper One, 2007), 83.

21. J. Pittman McGehee and Damon J. Thomas, *The Invisible Church: Finding Spirituality Where You Are* (Westport, Conn. Praeger, 2009), 7.

22. Ibid. 6–7.

23. See Dr. Martin Luther King Jr., Nobel Prize acceptance speech prize, Oslo, Norway, Devember 10, 1964.

24. Ibid.

3. THE CHURCH REVOLUTION

1. http://dictionary.reference.com/browse/revolution.

2. Ibid.

3. Jaroslav Pelikan, *The Vindication of Tradition*, Jefferson Lecture in the Humanities, 1983.

4. www.thesaurus.com/browse/tradition.

5. Bryant Myers, *Walking with the Poor: Principles and Practices of Transformational Development* (Maryknoll, N.Y.: Orbis, 1999), 44.

6. Robert C. Linthicum, *Empowering the Poor* (Monrovia, Calif.: MARC, 1991), 21–23.

7. Hope Yen, "New Census Milestone: Hispanics Reach 50 Million (March 24, 2011)," http://www.huffingtonpost.com/huff-wires/20110324/us-census-2010-population/.

8. Ken Blue, *Healing Spiritual Abuse: How to Break Free from Bad Church Experiences* (Downers Grove, Ill.: Intervarsity, 1993), 136–37.

9. Anne Rice, "Facebook profile," July 2010.

10. Ibid.

11. Christopher Hitchens, *god is Not Great: How Religion Poisons Everything* (New York: Twelve, 2007), 175.

12. Anne Lamott, "God Doesn't Take Sides," *Salon* (April 27, 2005), http://www.salon.com/news/opinion/feature/2005/04/27/gods_warning_signs/index.html.

13. Leonard Pitts, "Fed Up with Christianity, and with Good Reason," *Miami Herald* (Aug. 7, 2010), http://www.chron.com/disp/story.mpl/editorial/outlook/7144045.html.

14. Josiah Royce, *The Problem of Christianity* (Washington, D.C.: Catholic University of America Press, 2001), 265.

15. W. E. B. Dubois, *The Souls of Black Folks* (New York: Bantam, 1989), 3.

16. Pew Forum on Religion and Public Life, http://pewforum.org/A-Religious-Portrait-of-African-Americans.aspx.

17. Eddie Glaude Jr., "The Black Church Is Dead," *Huffington Post*, http://www.huffingtonpost.com/eddie-glaude-jr-phd/the-black-church-is-dead_b_473815.html (Feb. 24, 2010).

18. *National Urban League*, "State of Black America 2009: Message to the President," http://www.nul.org/newsroom/publications/soba, accessed July 27, 2011.

19. Leonard Pitts, (March 3, 2009). http://articles.cnn.com/2009-03-28/politics/pitts.black.america_1_non-hispanic-whites-post-racial-america-national-urban-league/2?_s=PM:POLITICS

20. Glaude, "The Black Church Is Dead." http://www.huffingtonpost.com/eddie-glaude-jr-phd/the-black-church-is-dead_b_473815.html

21. Ibid.

22. Ibid.

23. Ibid.

24. Robert Jensen, *All My Bones Shake: Seeking a Progressive Path to the Prophetic Voice* (Sydney, Australia: ReadHowYouWant, 2010), xix.

25. Richard Rohr, *Hope against Darkness: The Transforming Vision of Saint Francis in an Age of Anxiety* (Cincinnati: St. Anthony Messenger Press, 2001).

26. Tony Campolo, http://www.christianitytoday.com/le/2004/summer/3.54.html

27. "Marriages and Families in the Bible: Bible Passages Describing Eight Famiily/Marriage Types," http://www.religioustolerance.org/mar_bibl0.htm, accessed July 31, 2011.

28. J. Pittman McGehee and Damon J. Thomas, *The Invisible Church* (Westport, Conn.: Praeger, 2009), 50–52.

29. Loren Mead, *The Once and Future Church Collection* (Bethesda, Md.: Alban Institute, 2001), 14.

4. FROM THE EDGE

1. Gil Rendle, *Journey in the Wilderness* (Nashville: Abingdon, 2010), 96.

2. Ibid., 100.

3. Seth Godin, *Tribes: We Need You to Lead Us* (New York: Portfolio, 2008), 96.

4. Ibid., 11.

5. Matt Miller, *The Tyranny of Dead Ideas: Letting Go of the Old Ways of Thinking to Unleash a New Prosperity* (New York: Times Books, 2009).

6. David Putman, *Detox: For the Overly Religious* (Nashville: B & H Publishing Group, 2010), xv.

7. Godin, *Tribes*, 81.

8. Ibid., 82.

9. Thomas G. Bandy, *Coaching Change: Breaking Down Resistance, Building Up Hope* (Nashville: Abingdon, 2000), 163–77.

10. Ibid., 172.

11. Leonard Sweet, *So Beautiful, Devine Design for Life and the Church* (Colorado Springs: David C. Cook, 2009), 35–40.

12. Ibid., 36.

13. Ibid., 18.

14. Michael Frost and Alan Hirsch, *The Shaping of Things to Come: Innovation and Mission for the Twenty-first-Century Church* (Peabody, Mass.: Hendrickson; Erina, New South Wales, Australia, 2003), 41.

15. Dr. Joseph W. Daniels Jr., *Begging for Real Church* (Washington, DC, Beacon of Light Resources, 2009), 37.

16. Ibid., 41.

17. Diana Butler Bass, *The Practicing Congregation: Imagining a New Old Church* (Herndon, Va.: Alban Institute, 2004), 35.

18. Rory Noland, *The Heart of the Artist: A Character-building Guide for You and Your Ministry Team* (Grand Rapids: Zondervan, 1999), 29.

19. Richard Florida, *The Rise of the Creative Class: And How It's Transforming Word, Leisure, Community and Everyday Life* (New York: Basic), xxvii.

20. Ibid.

21. Ibid., xxix–xxx.

22. Leonard Sweet, *Nudge: Awakening Each Other to the God Who's Already There* (Colorado Springs: David C. Cook, 2010), 16.

23. Rendle, *Journey in the Wilderness*, 100.

24. Florida, *The Rise of the Creative Class*, 31.

25. Iain McGilchrist, *The Master and His Emissary* (New Haven, Conn.: Yale University Press, 2009).

26. Daniel H. Pink, *A Whole New Mind: Why Right-Brainers Will Rule the Future* (New York: Riverhead, 2006), 3.

27. Ibid., 26.

28. Ibid., 27.

29. Michael J. Mauboussin, *Think Twice: Harnessing the Power of Counterintuition* (Boston: Harvard Business Press, 2009), 3–4.

30. Ibid., 4.

31. Ibid., 3–16.

32. Seth Godin, *Small Is the New Big: And 183 Other Riffs, Rants, and Remarkable Business Ideas* (New York: Penguin, 2006).

33. Godin, *Tribes*, 52.

34. Florida, *The Rise of the Creative Class*, 381–82.

35. Ibid., 382.

36. William C. Taylor and Polly LaBarre, *Mavericks at Work: Why the Most Original Minds in Business Win* (New York: William Morrow, 2006), 9.

37. Nadia Bolz-Weber, *Salvation on the Small Screen? Twenty-four Hours of Christian Television* (New York: Seabury, 2008), 3.

38. Taylor and LaBarre, *Mavericks at Work*, 96–97.

39. Jim Collins, *How the Mighty Fall: And Why Some Companies Never Give In* (New York: Jim Collins; distributed by Harper Collins, 2009), 97.

40. Howard Schultz, *Onward: How Starbucks Fought for Its Life without Losing Its Soul* (New York: Rodale, 2011), 6, 13.

41. Ibid., 13.

42. Ibid., 32.

43. Ibid., 66–67.

44. Ibid., 83.

45. N. T. Wright, *Surprised by Hope: Rethinking Heaven, the Resurrection, and the Mission of the Church* (New York: HarperCollins, 2008), 259.

46. "Scarred and Battered," in *The Collected Poems of Langston Hughes*, ed. Arnold Rampersad (New York: Vintage, 1994), 295.

CPSIA information can be obtained at www.ICGtesting.com
Printed in the USA
LVOW030354291211

261469LV00004B/2/P